Boys Coloring Book: Airplane & Helicopter

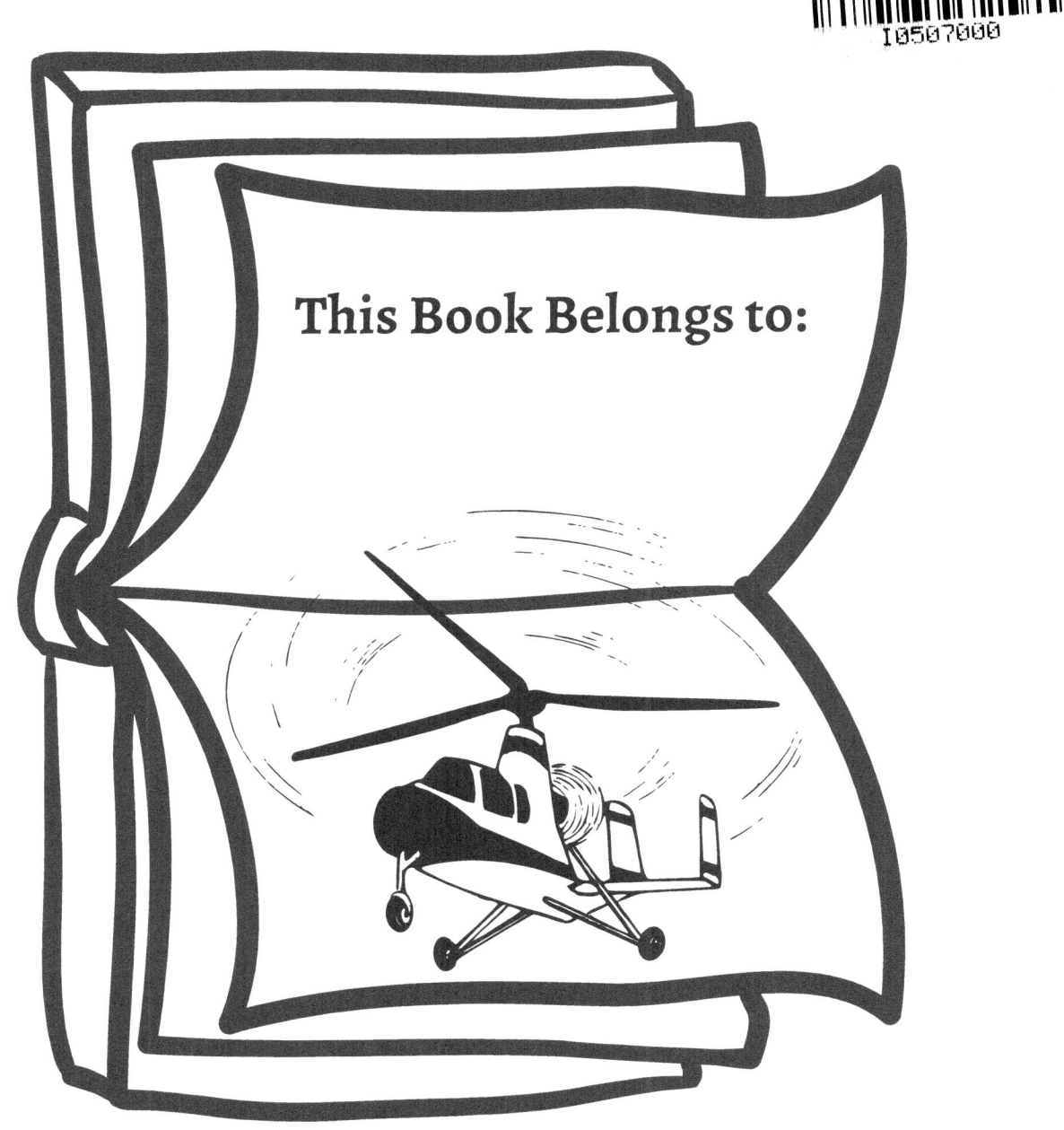

This Book Belongs to:

Copyright © 2020 by L. Farrell Publishing. All Rights Reserved.

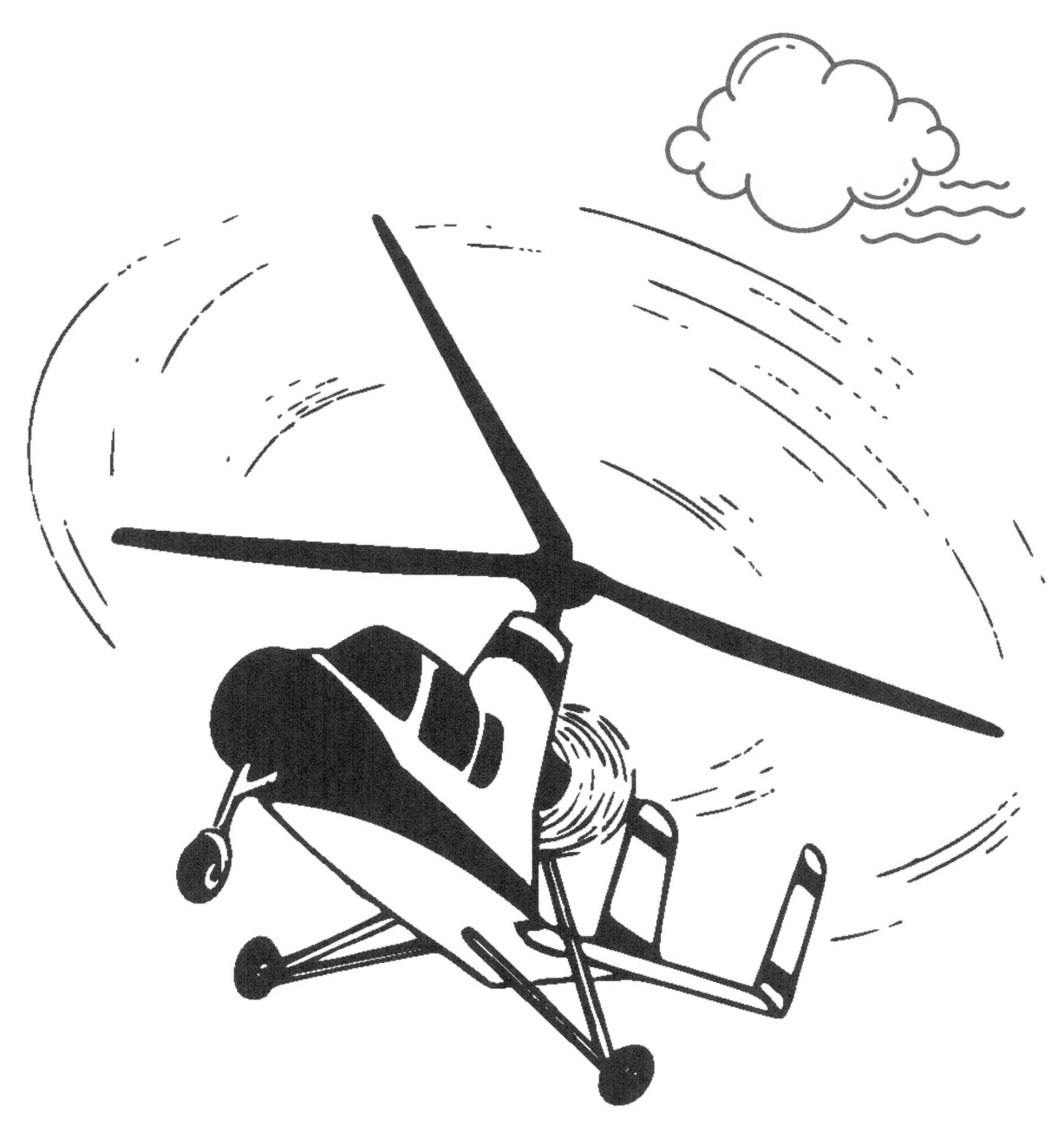

1

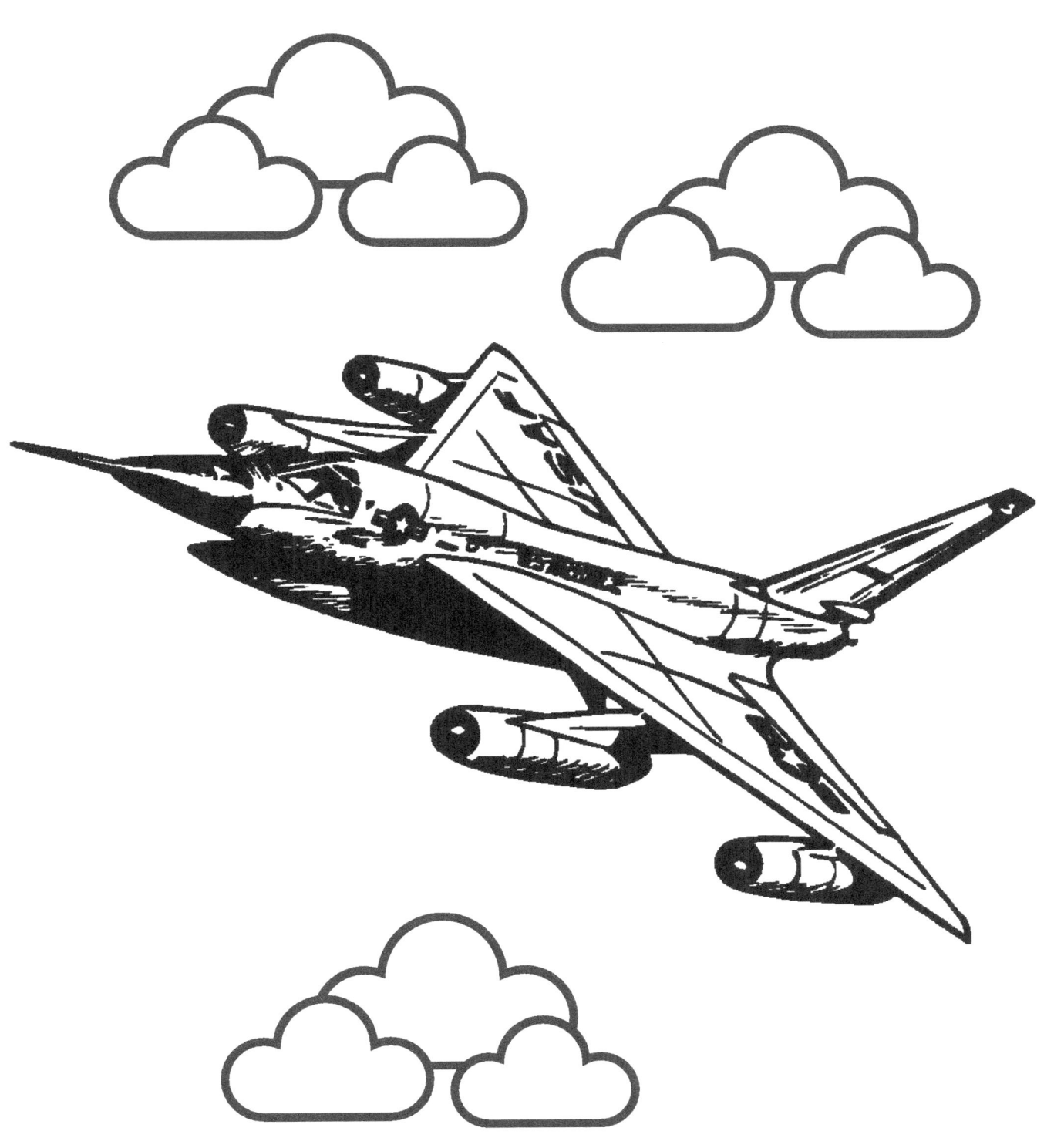

2

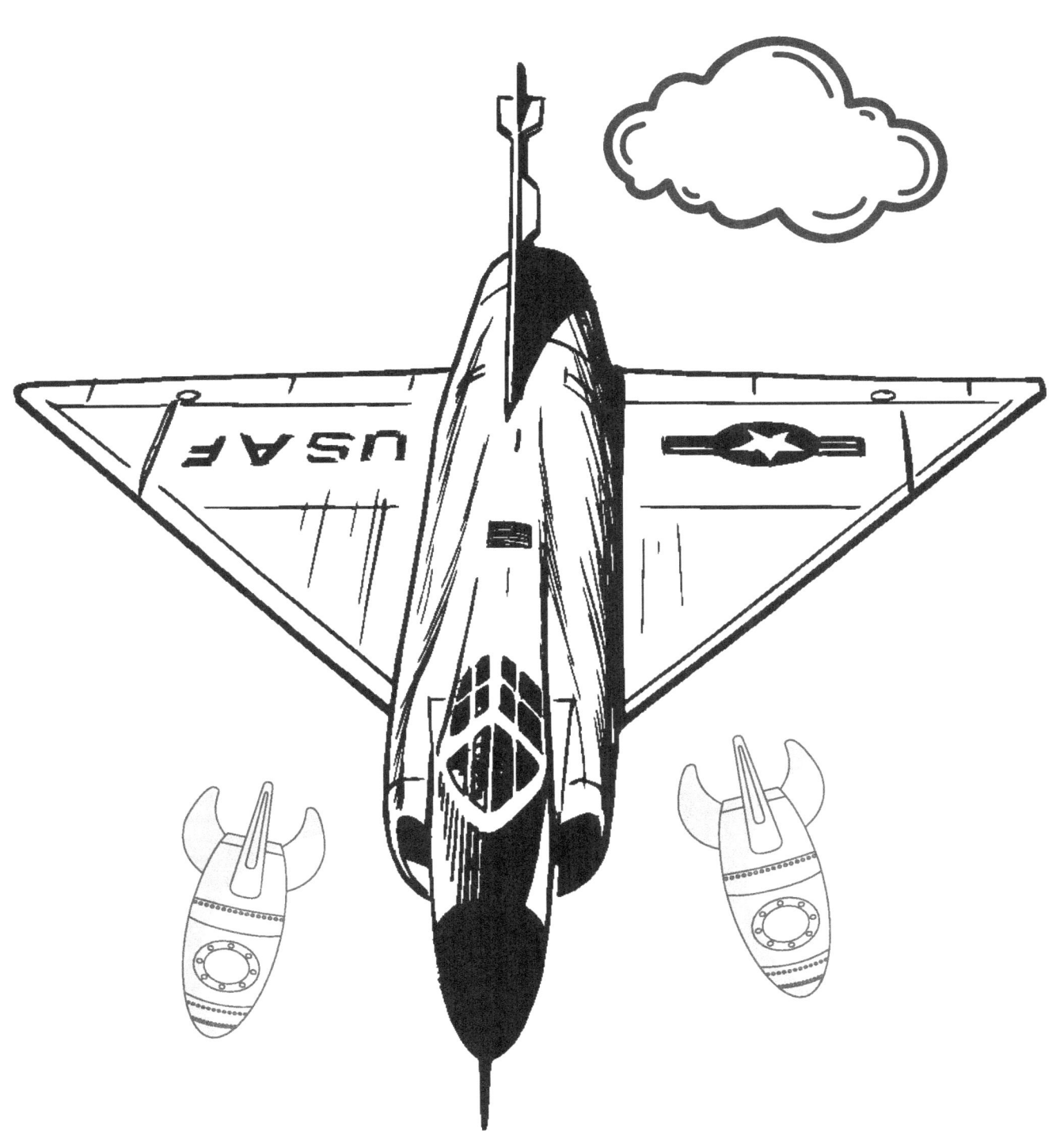

3

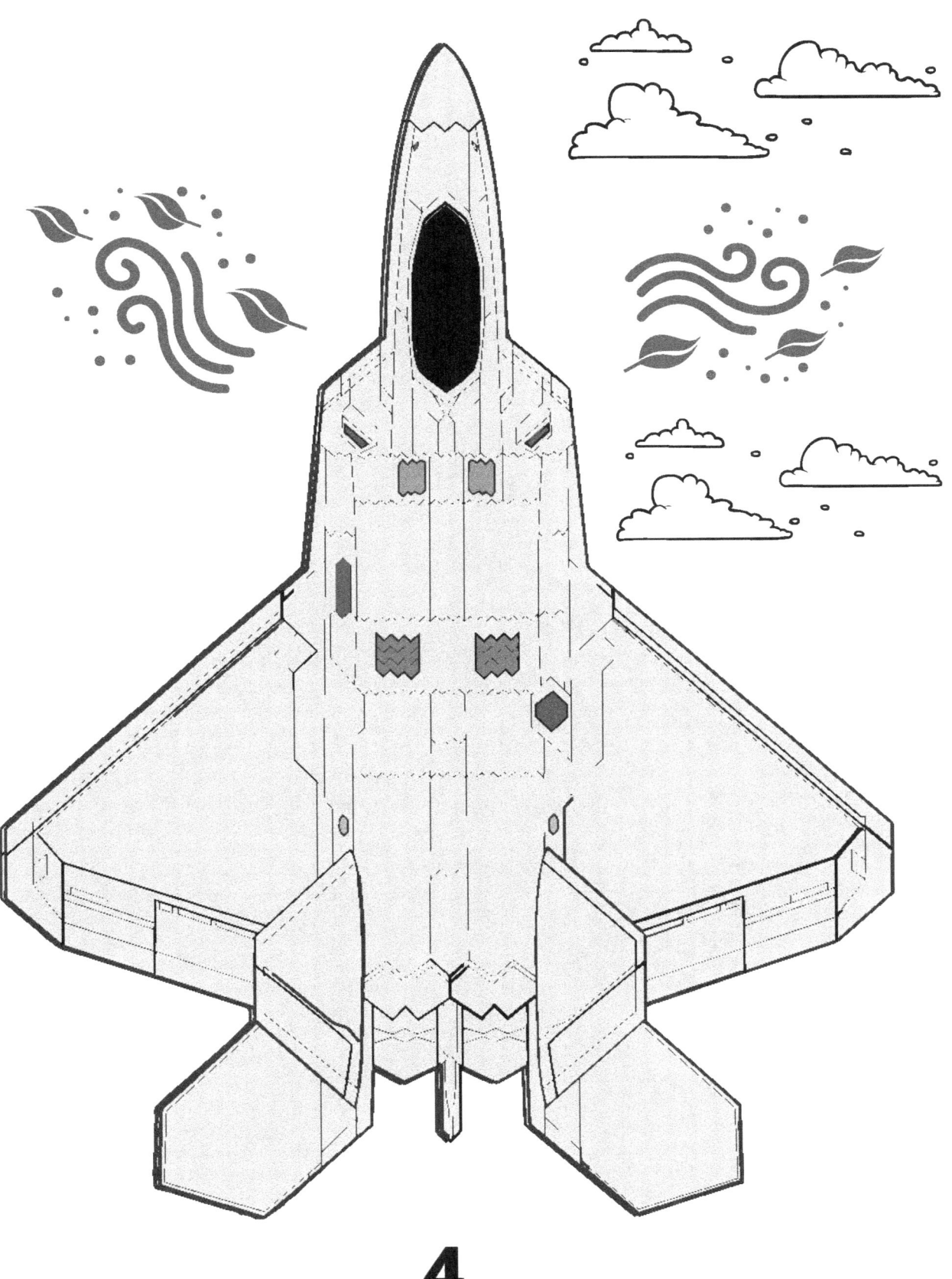

4

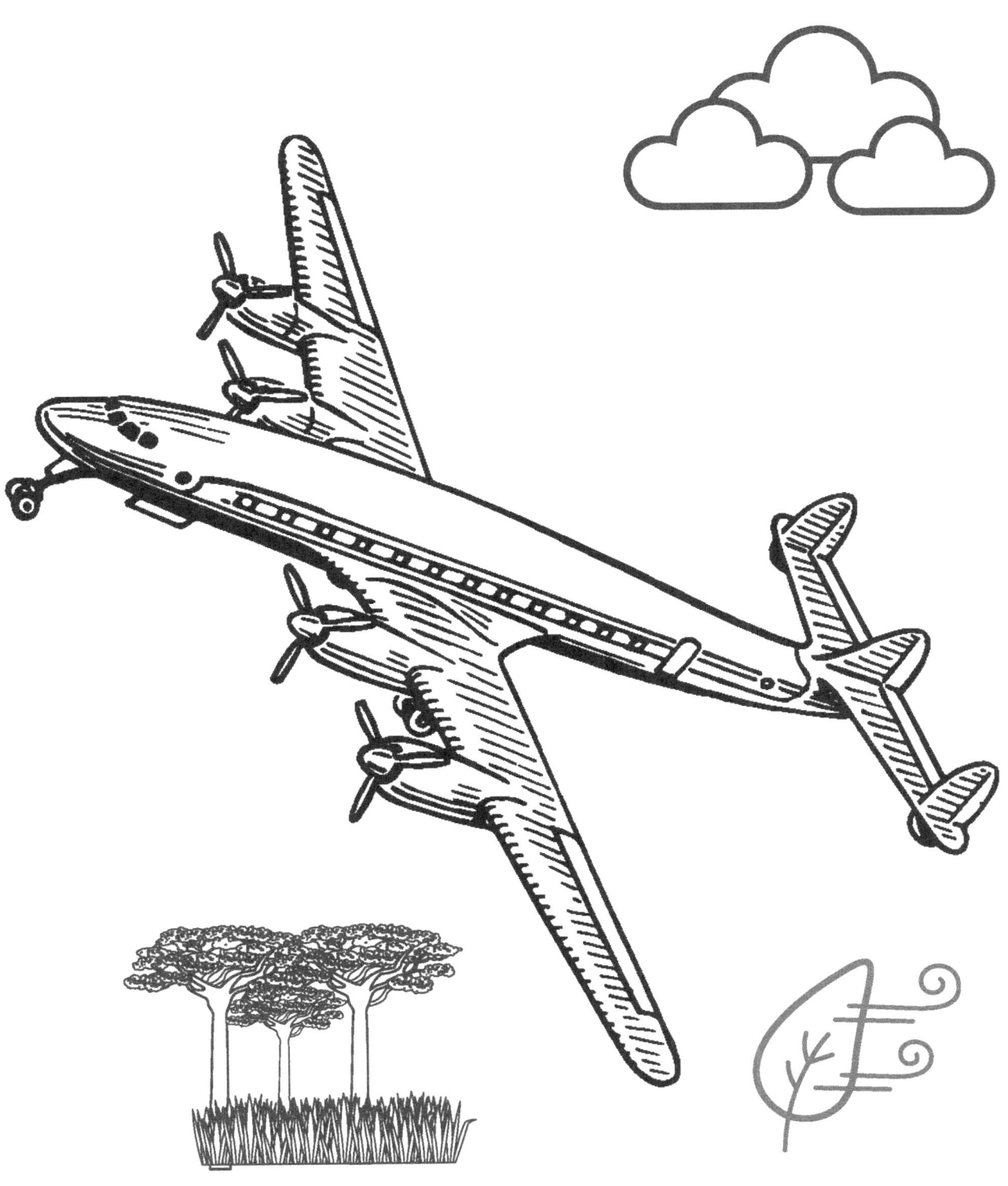

5

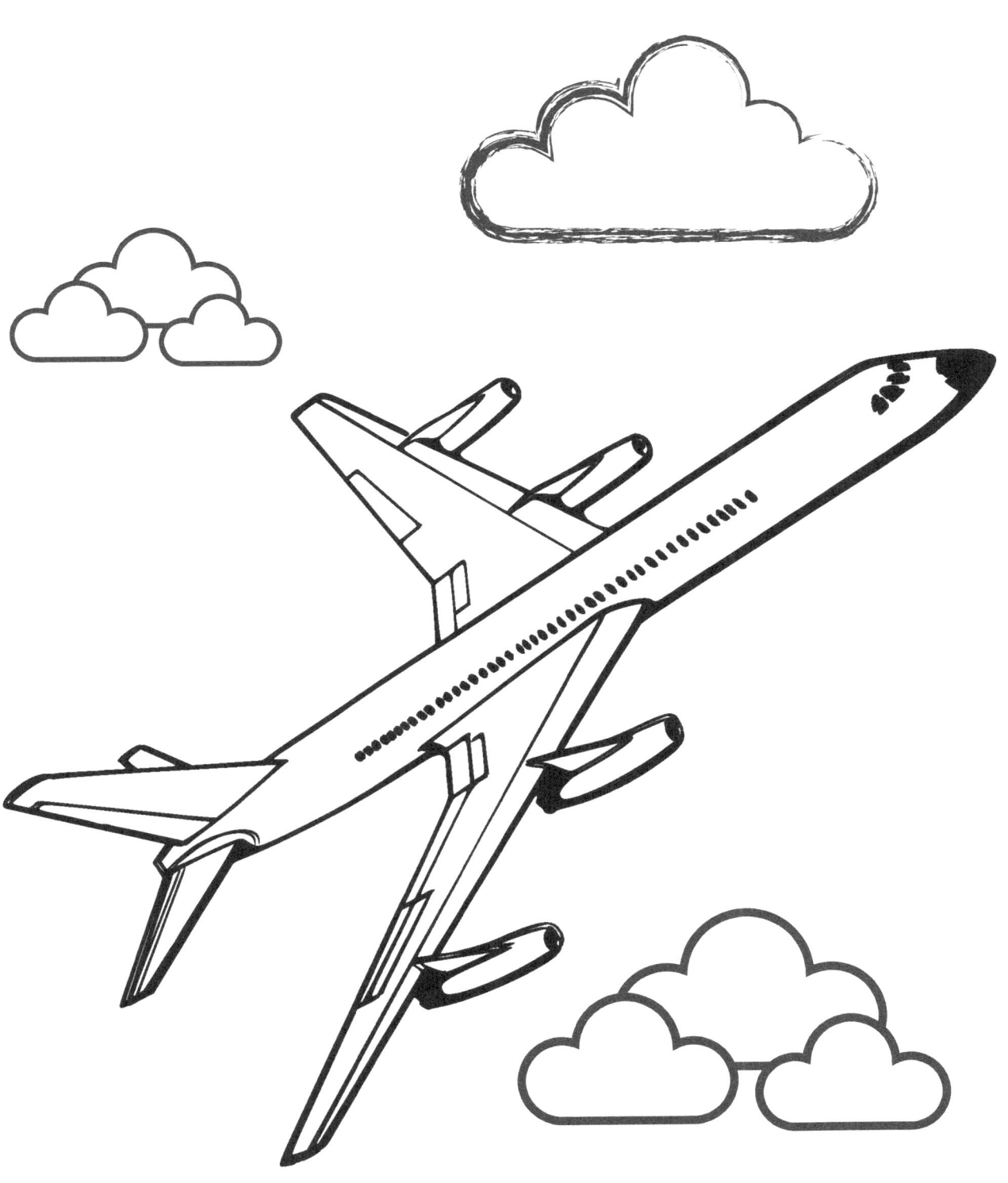

6

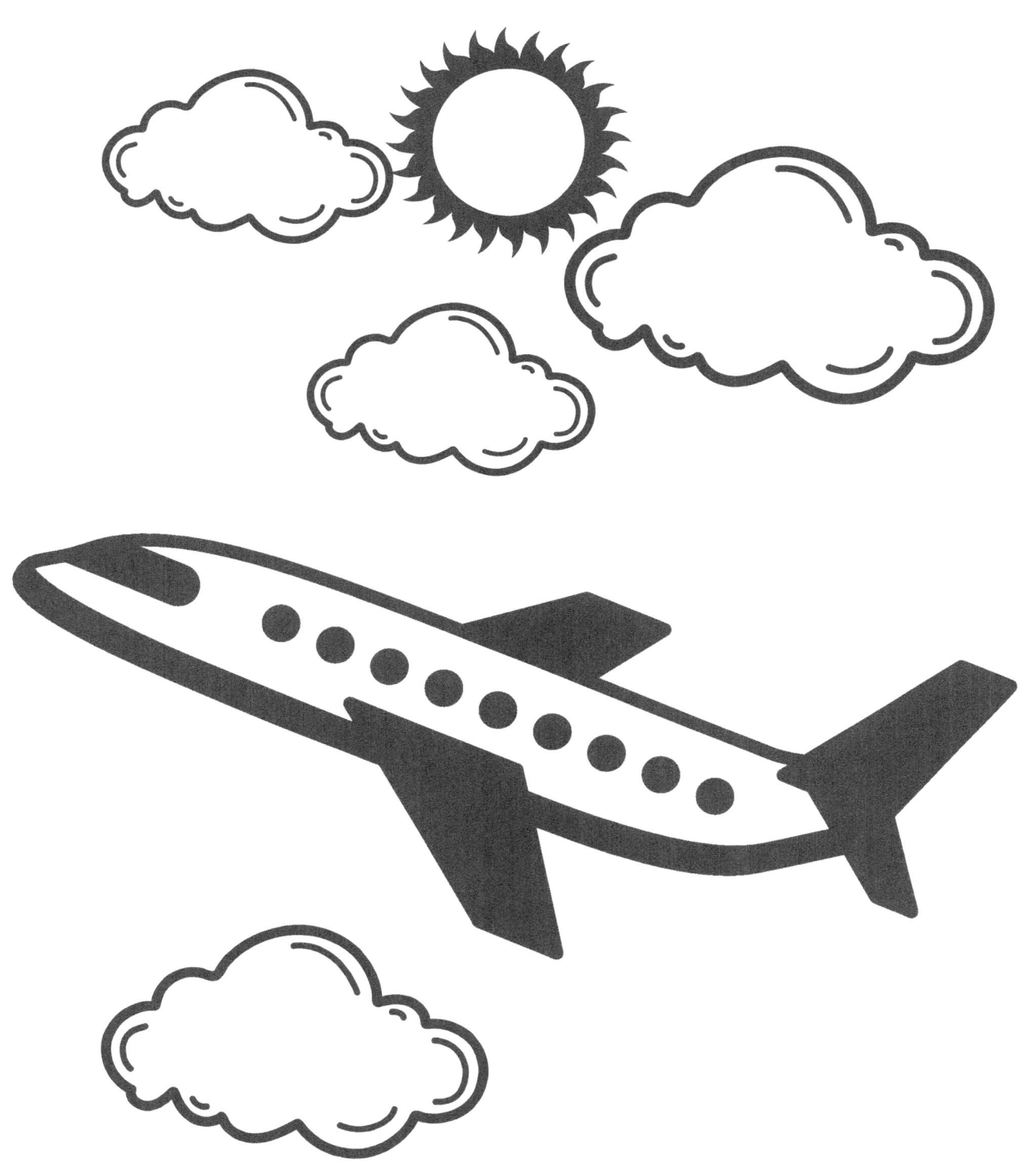

7

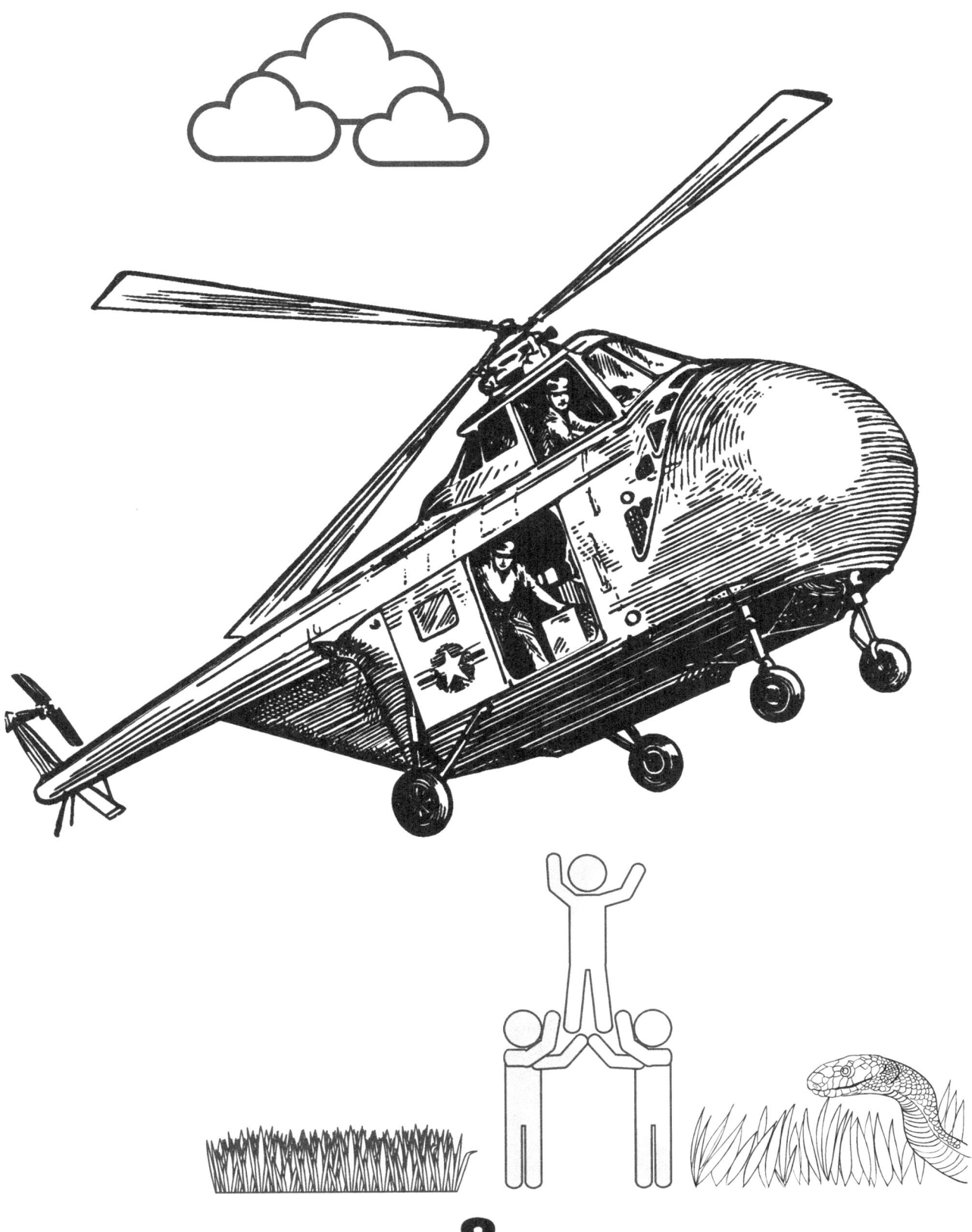

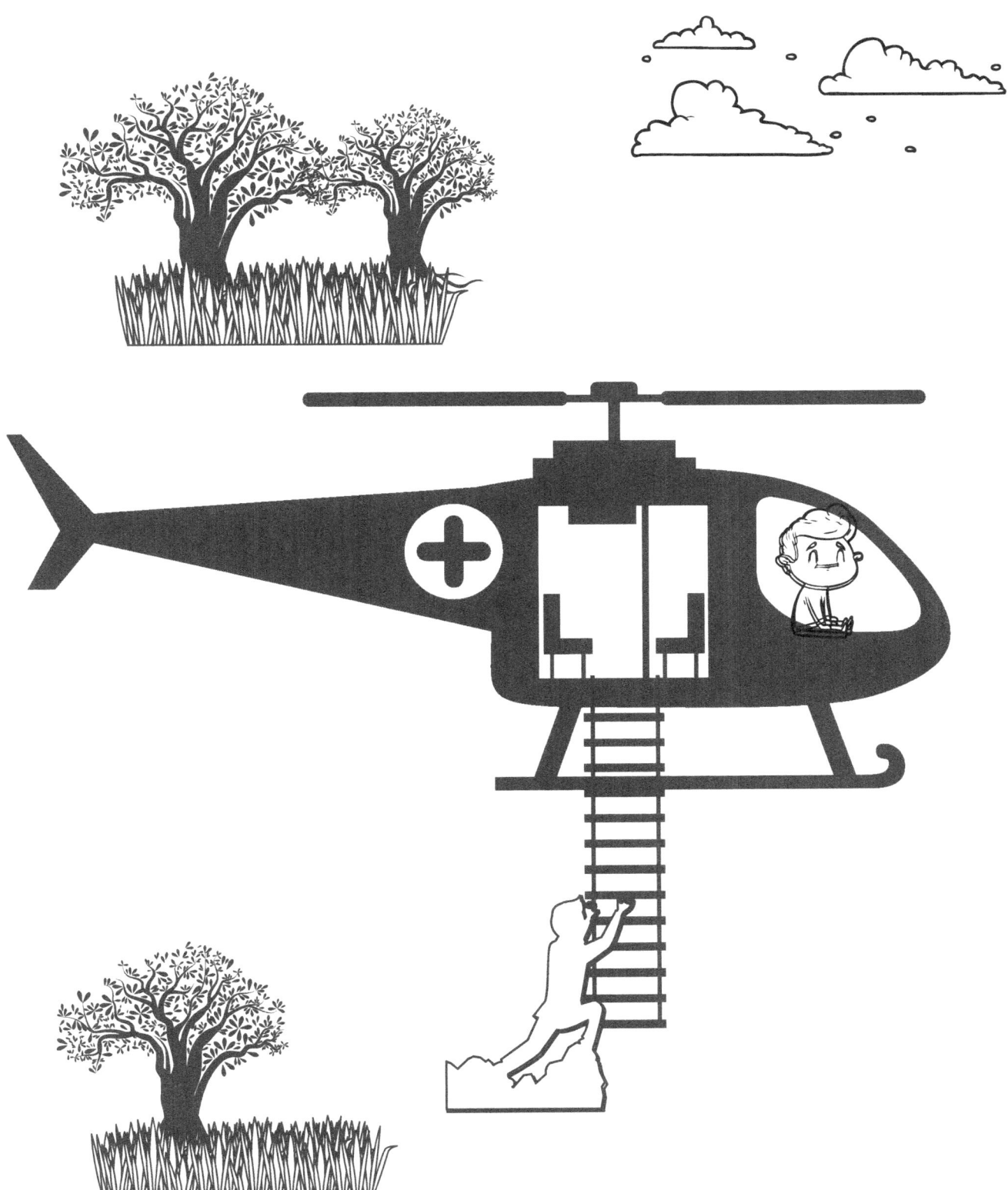

9

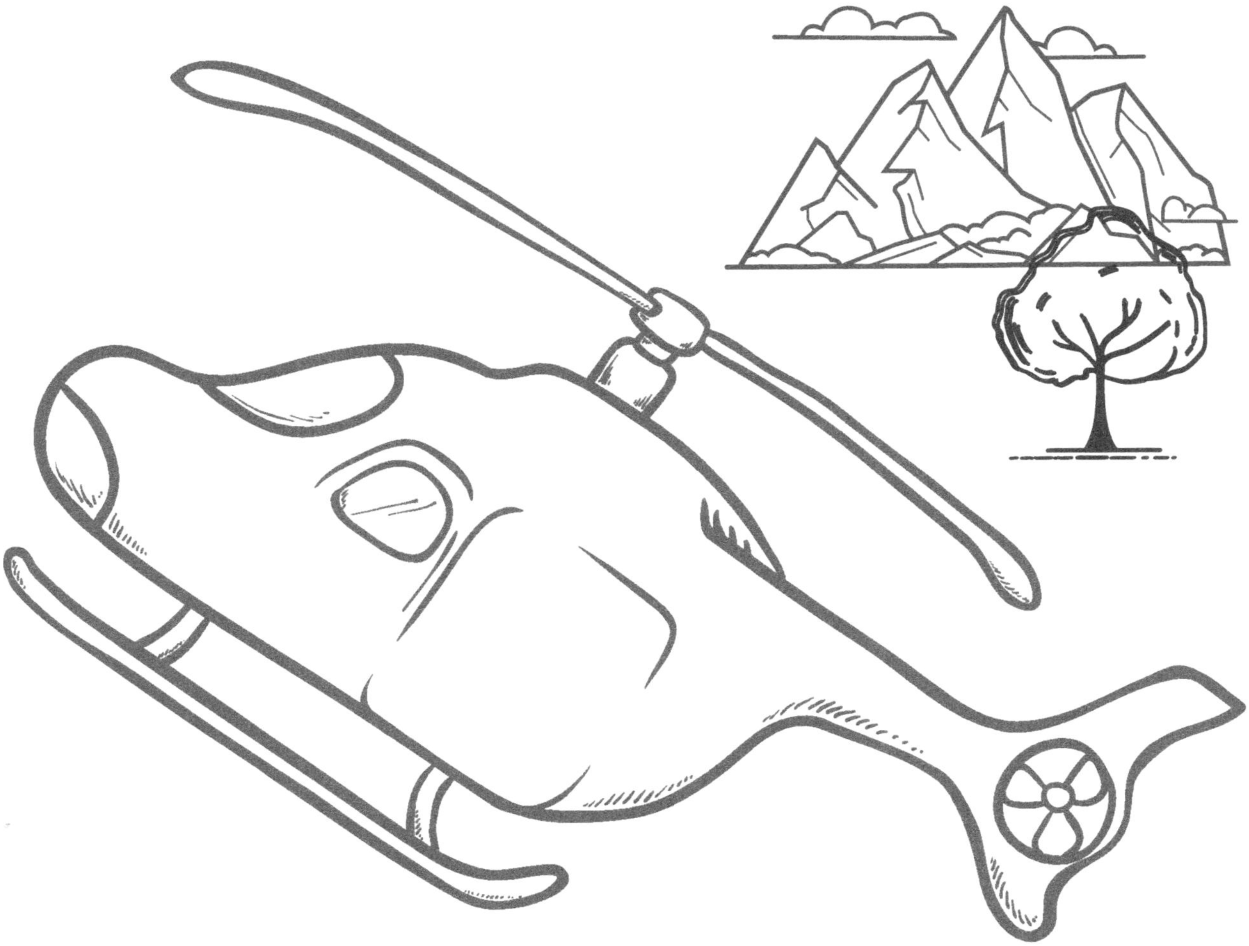

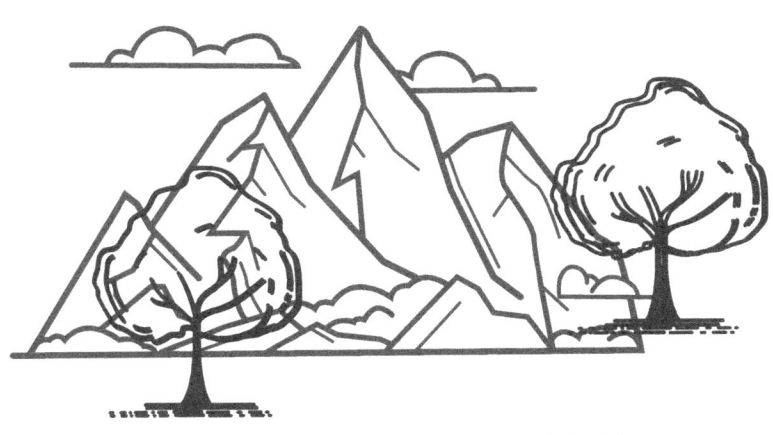

10

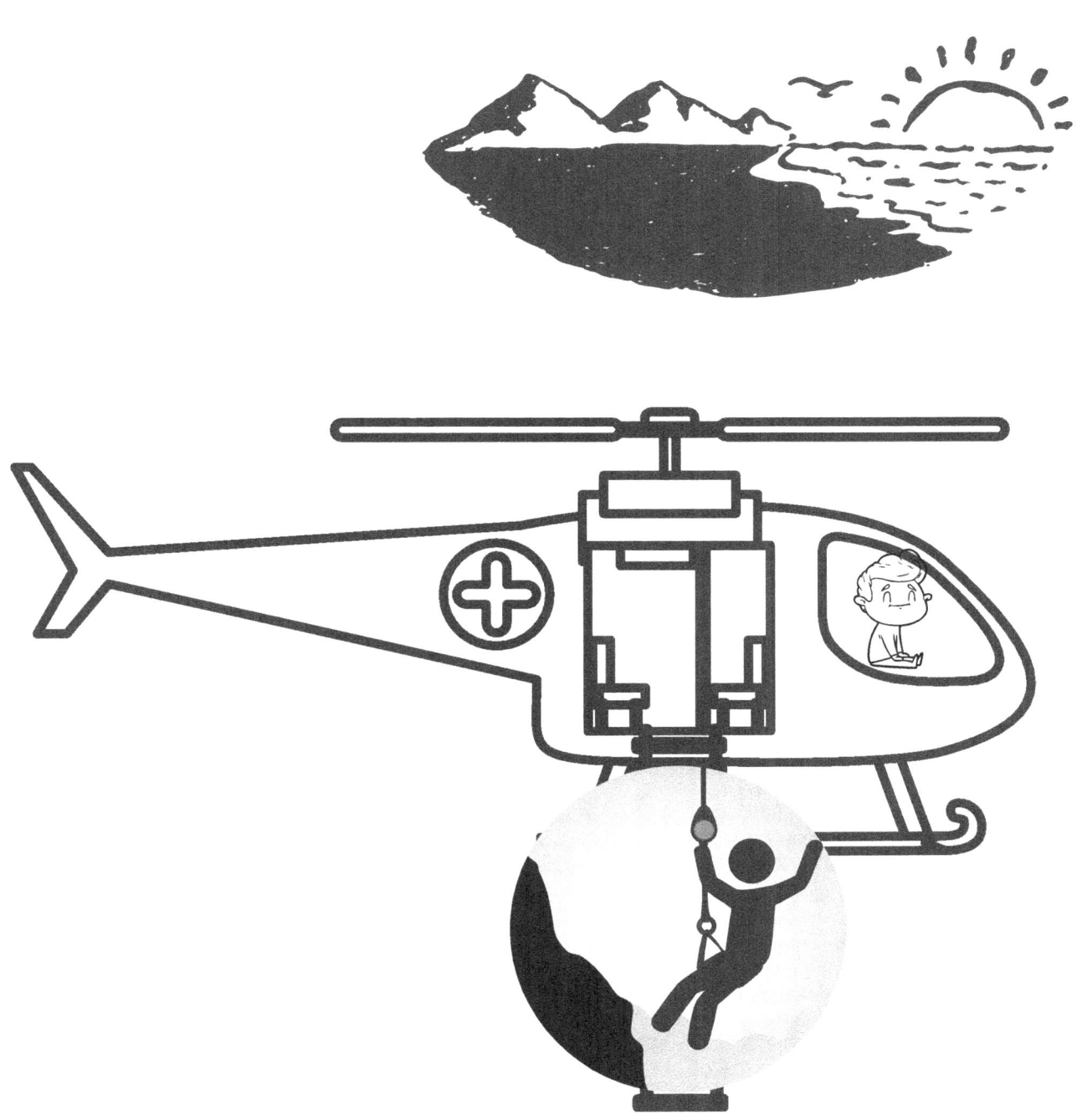

11

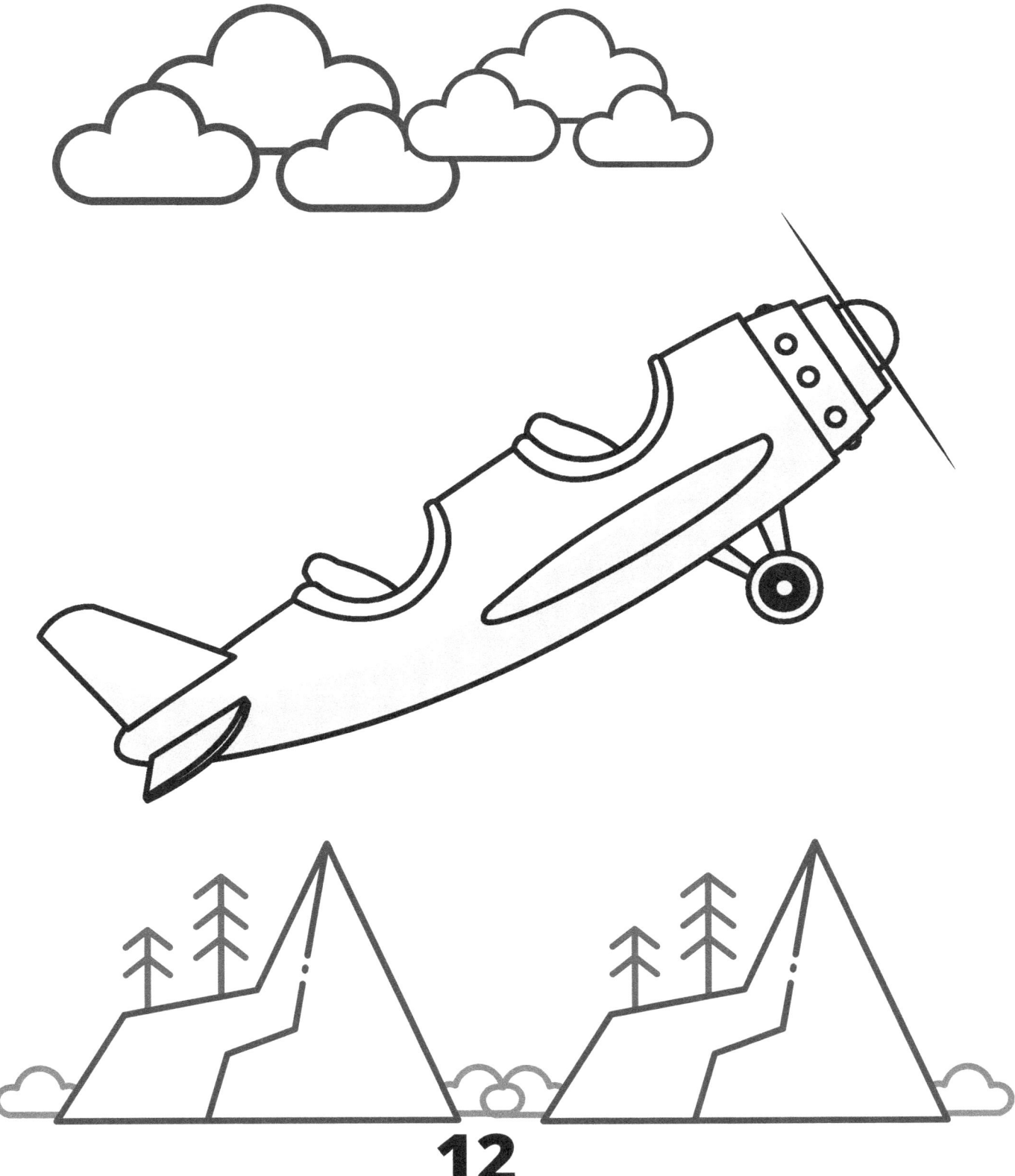

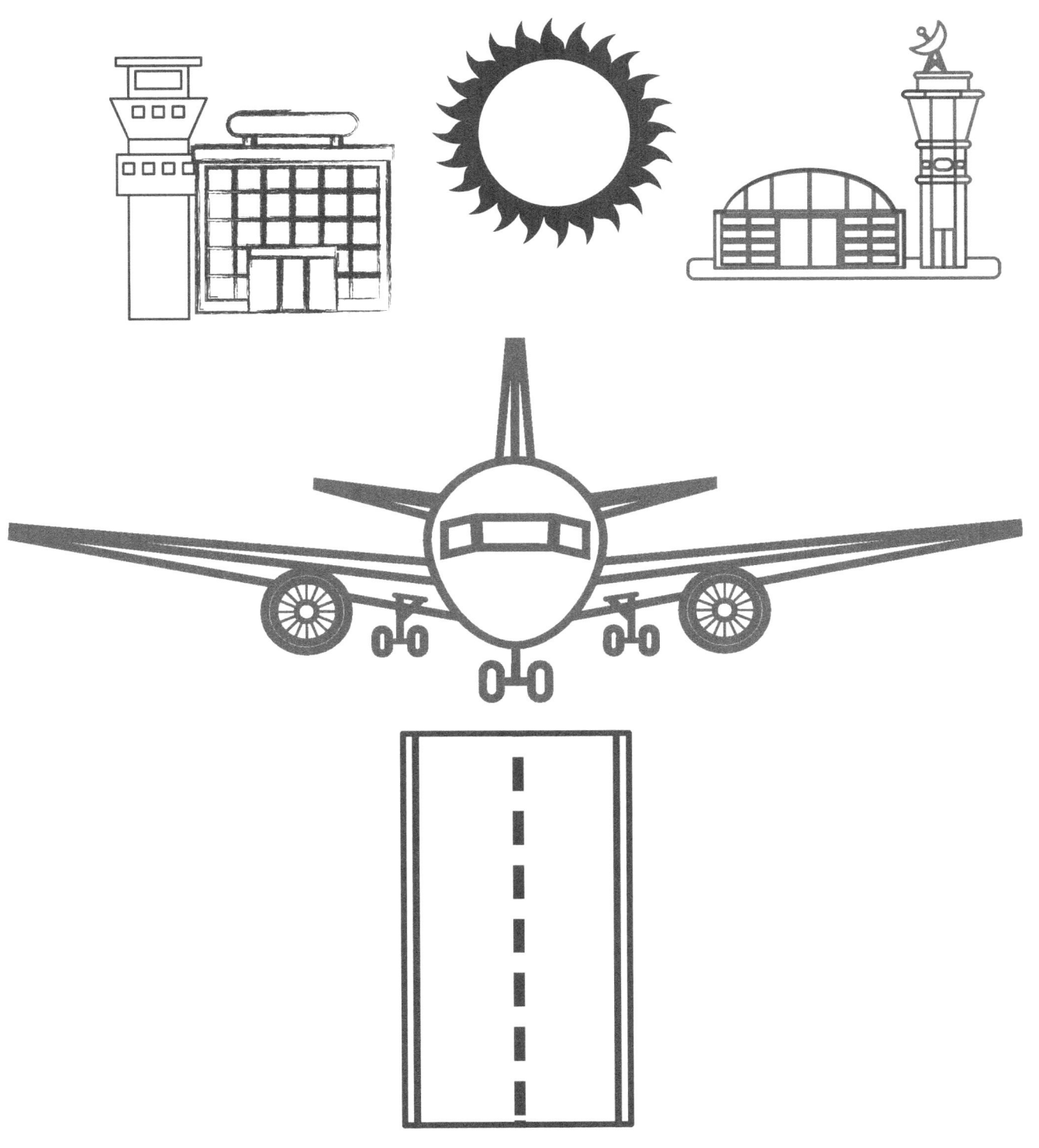

13

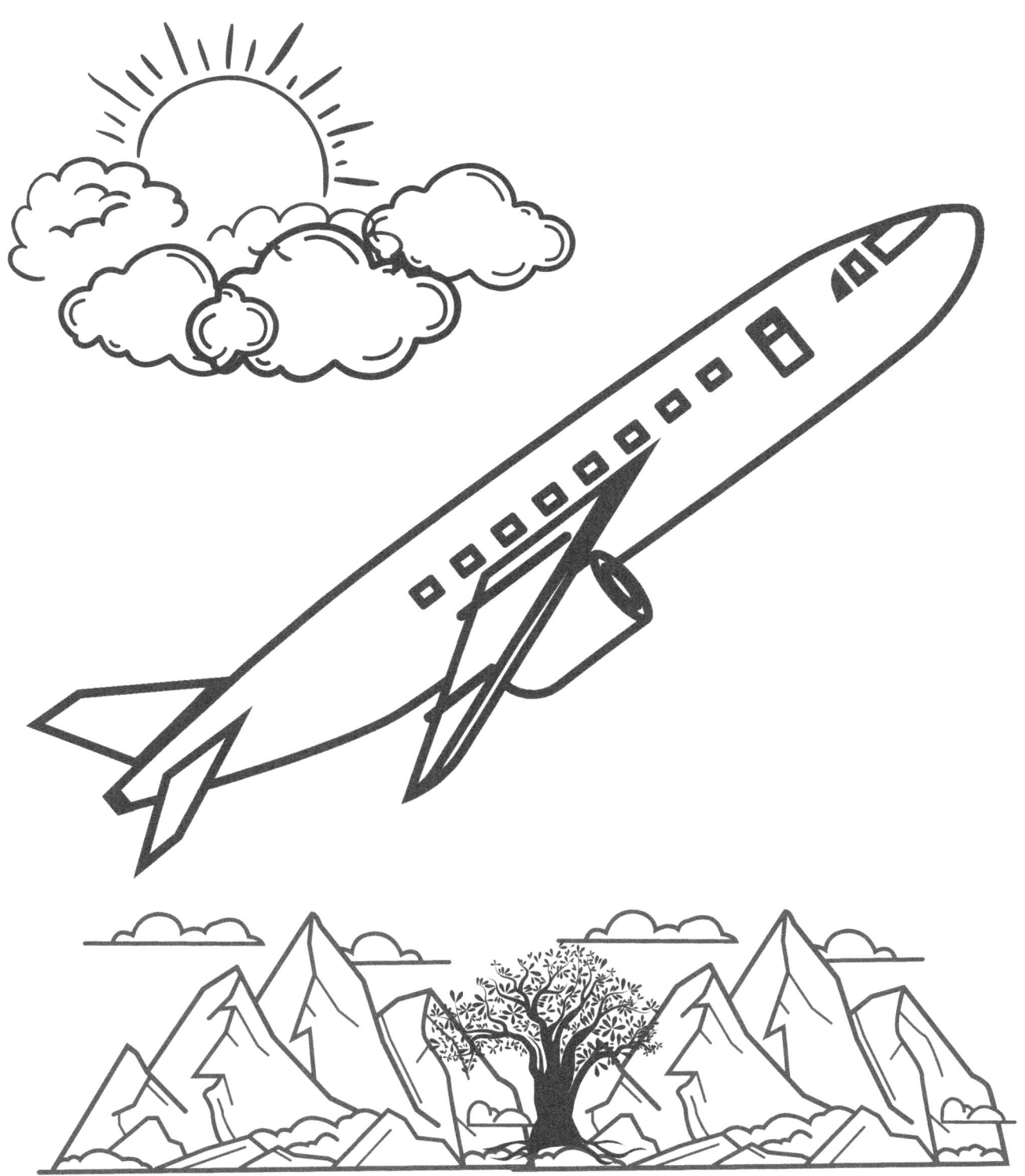

14

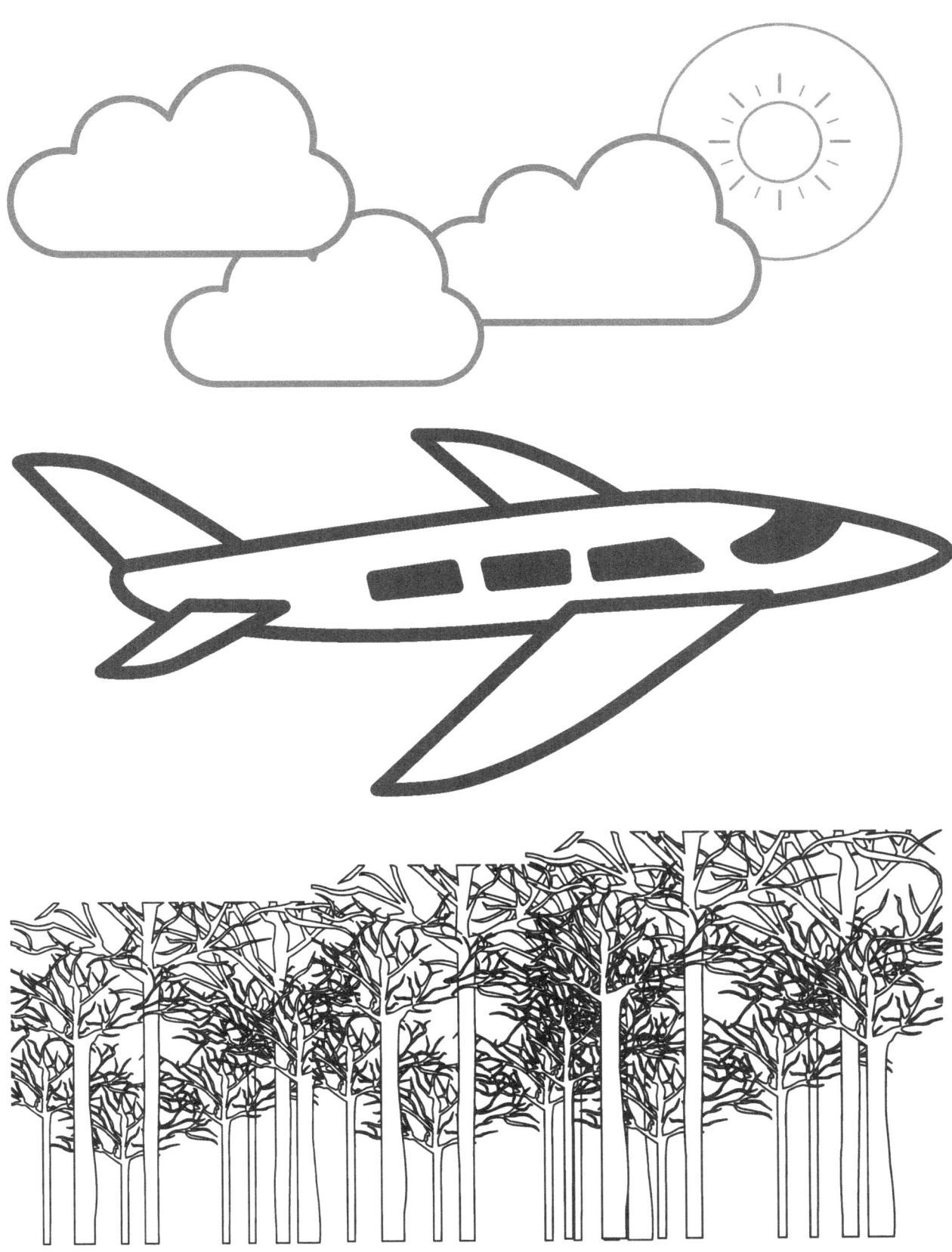

15

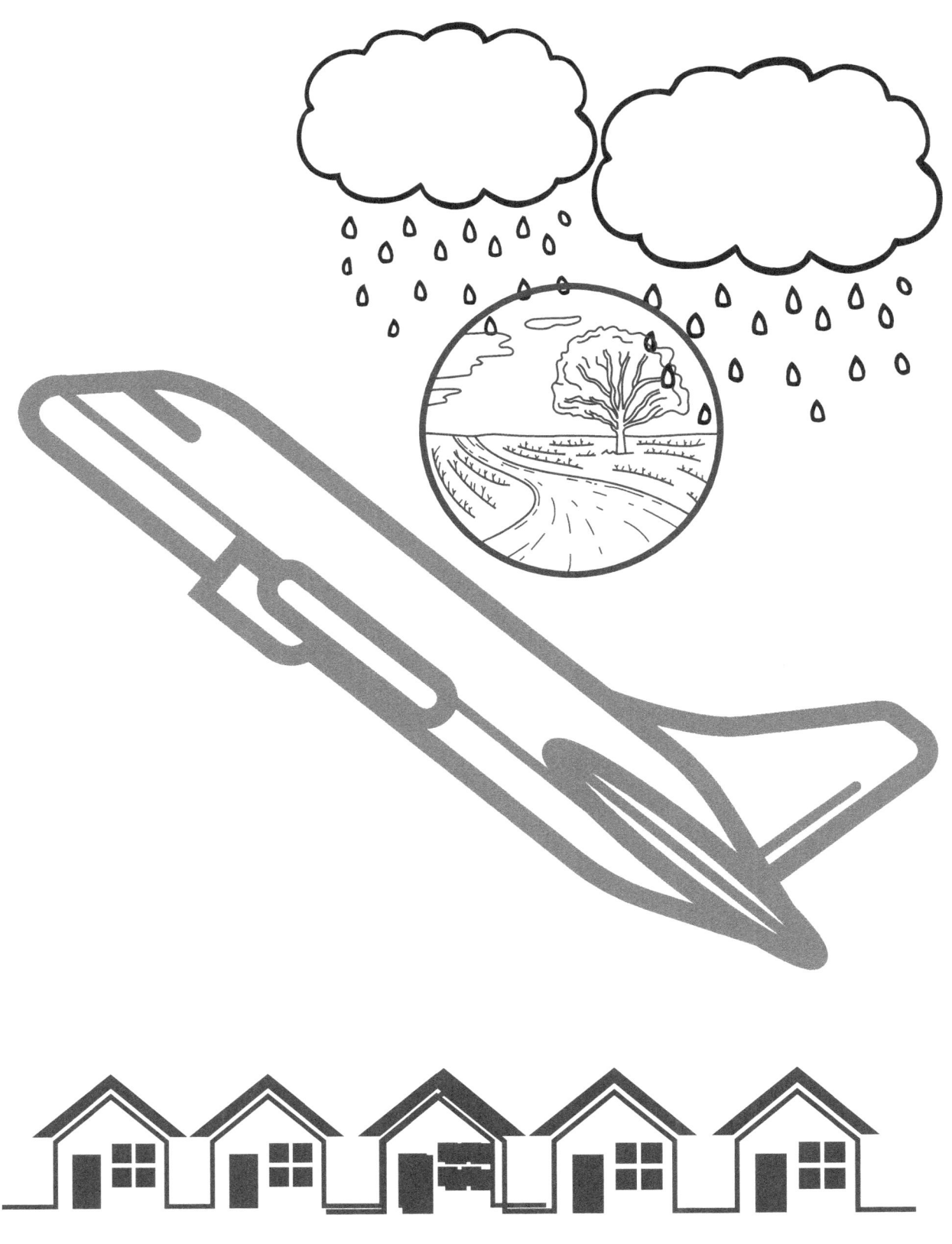

16

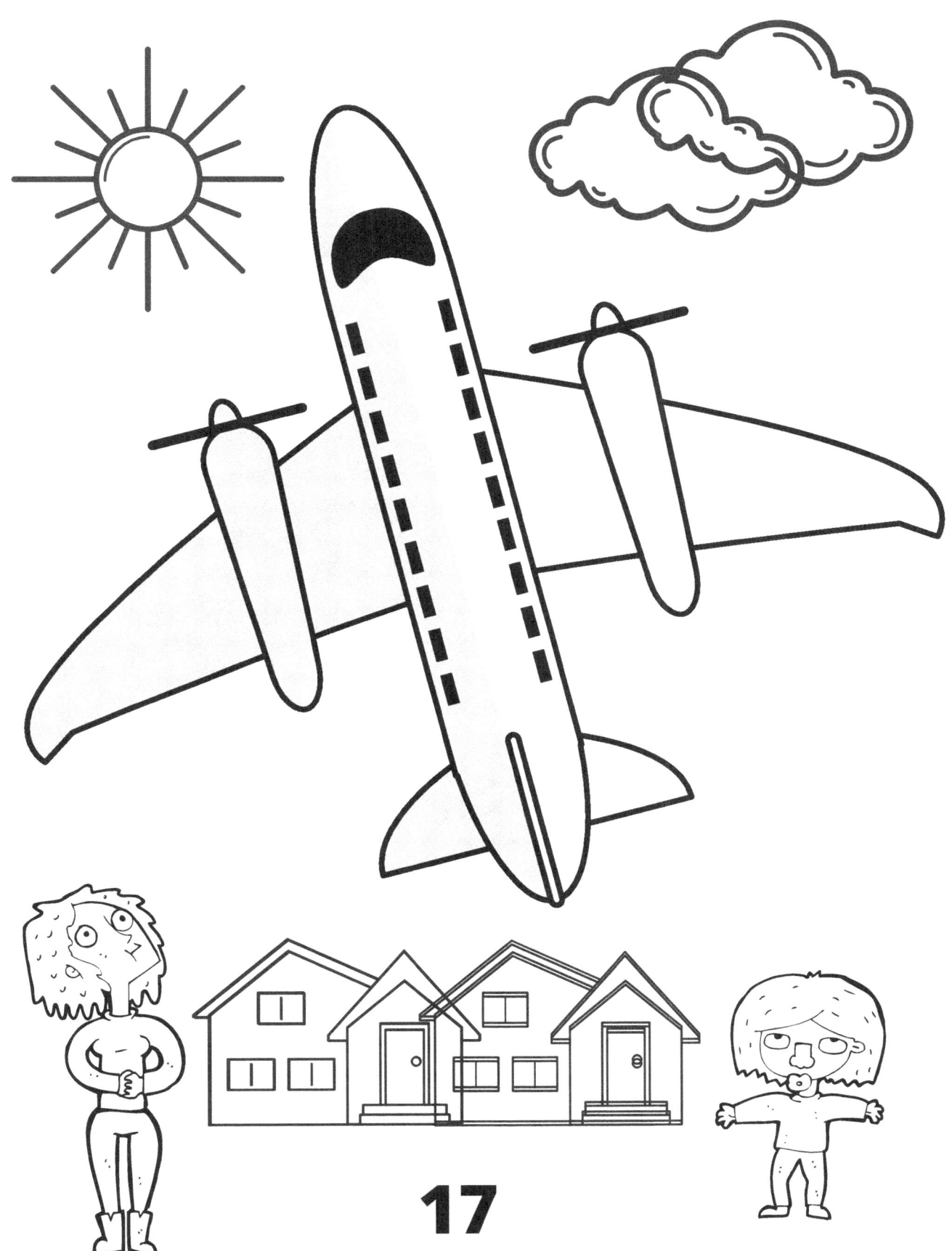

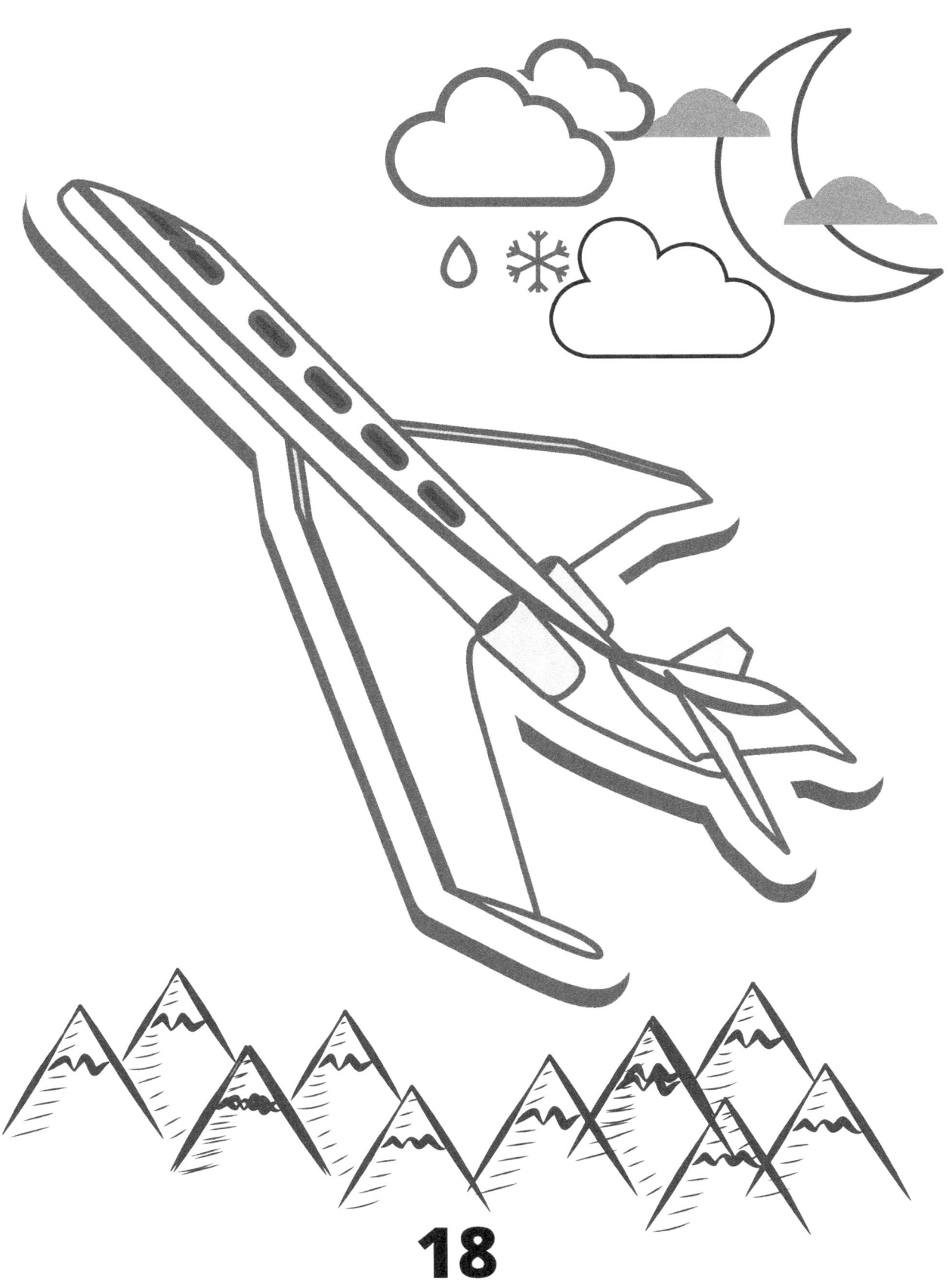

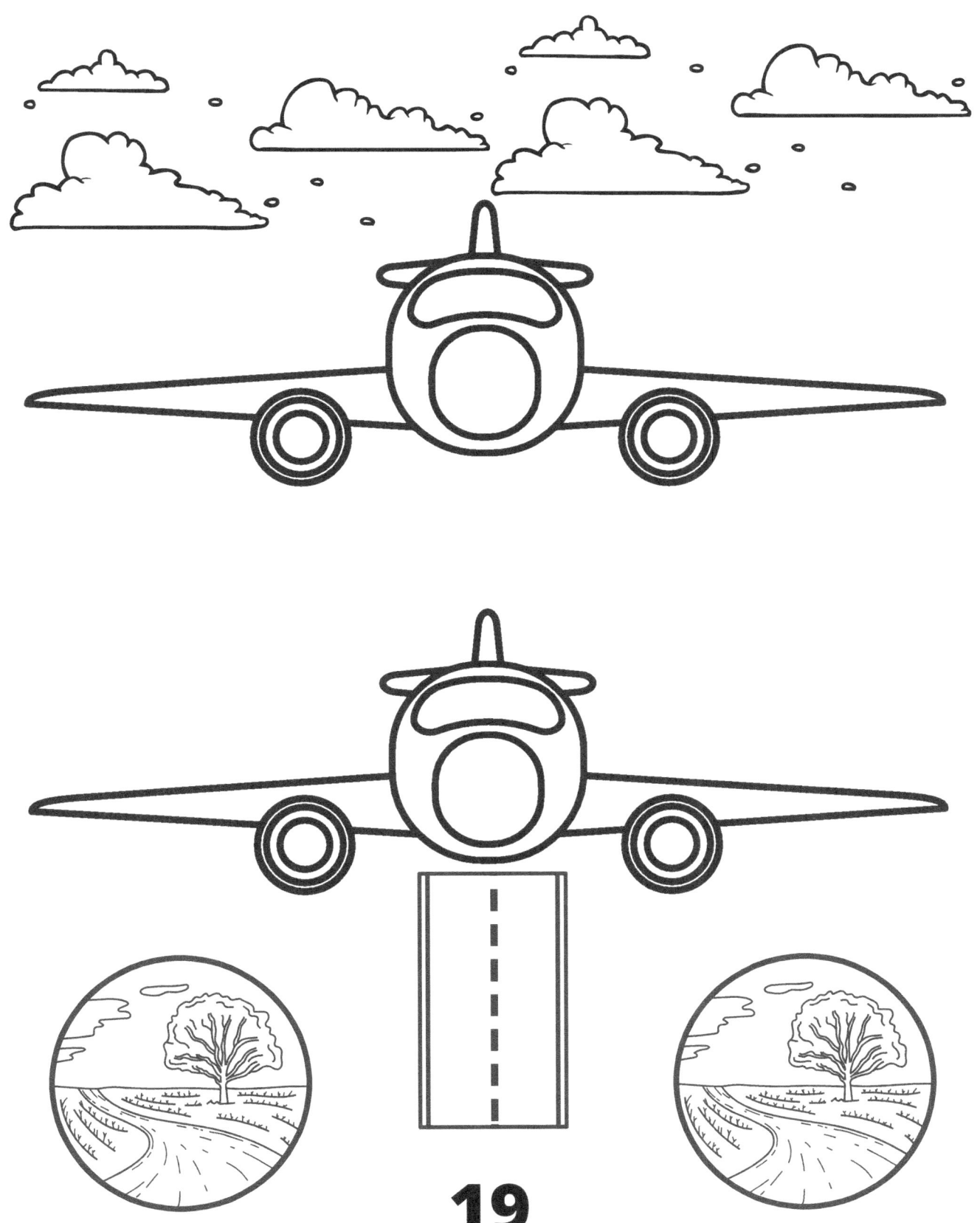

19

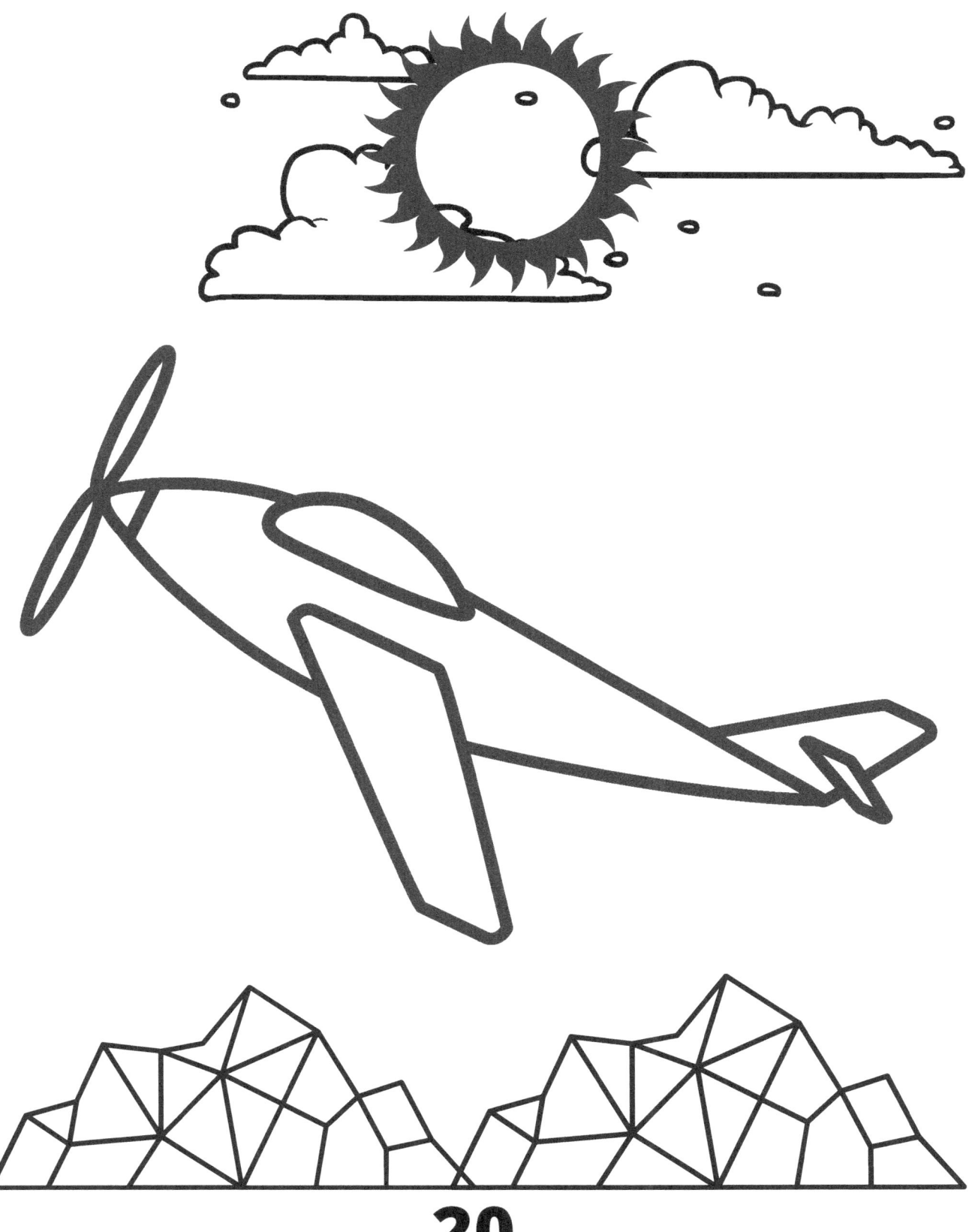

20

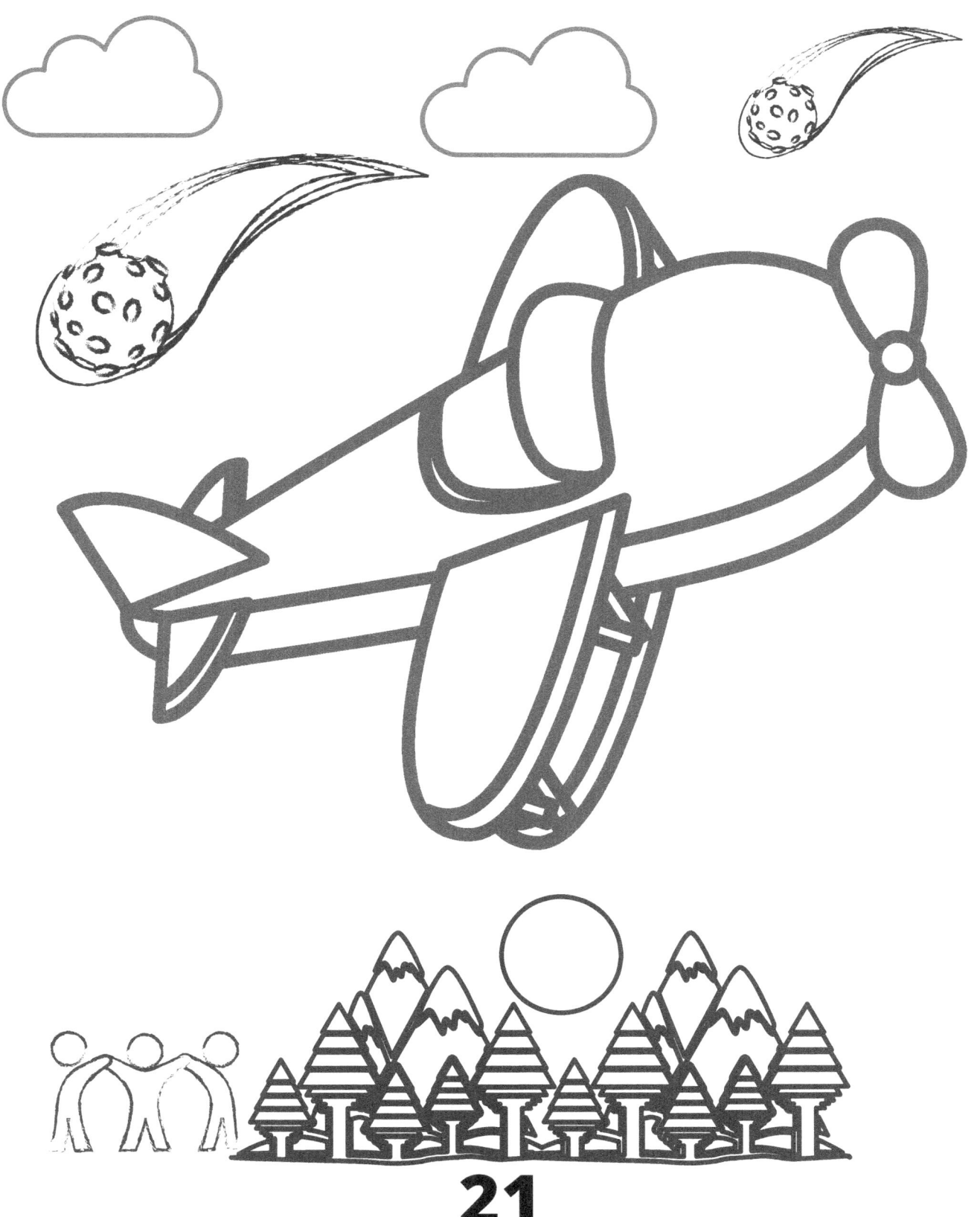

21

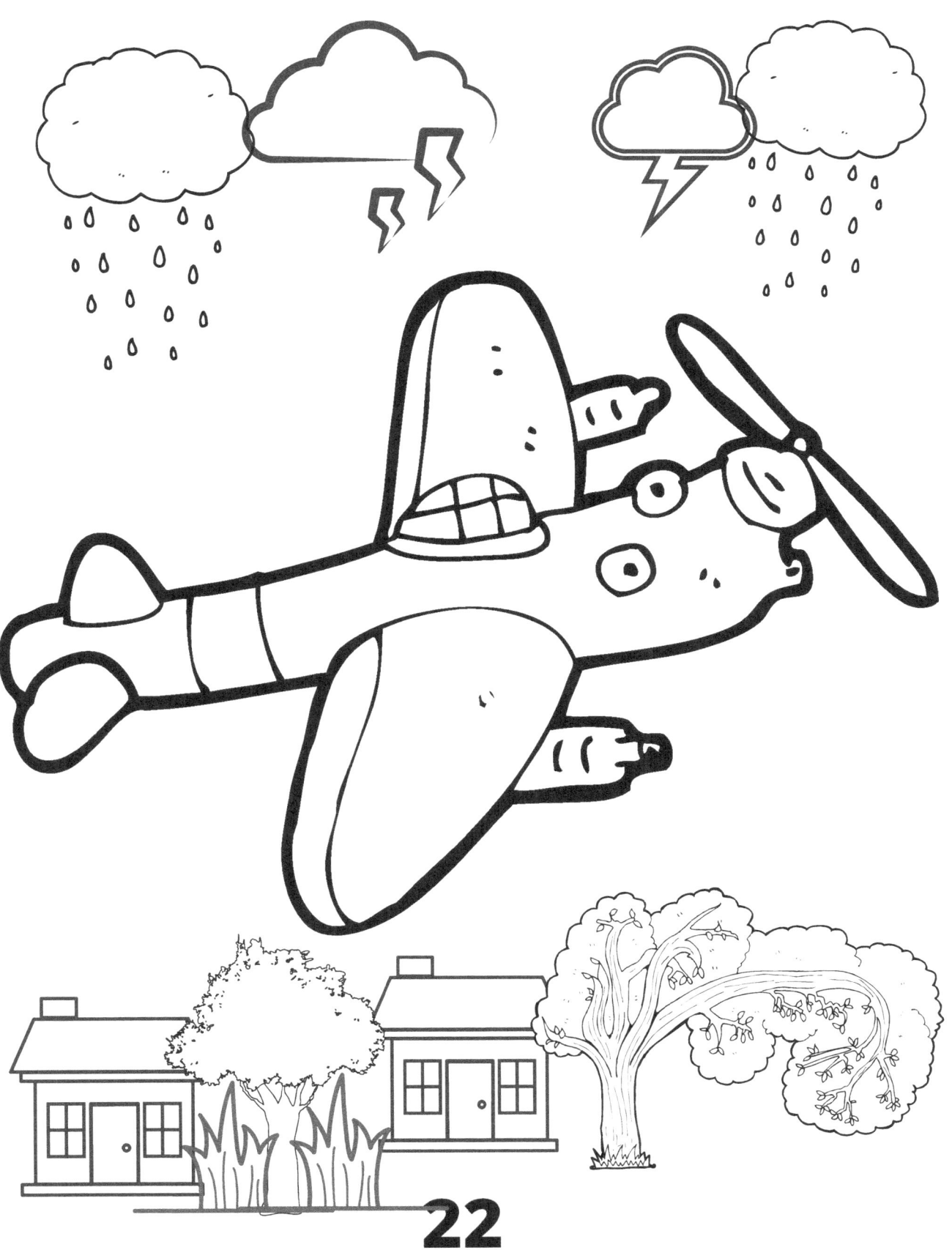

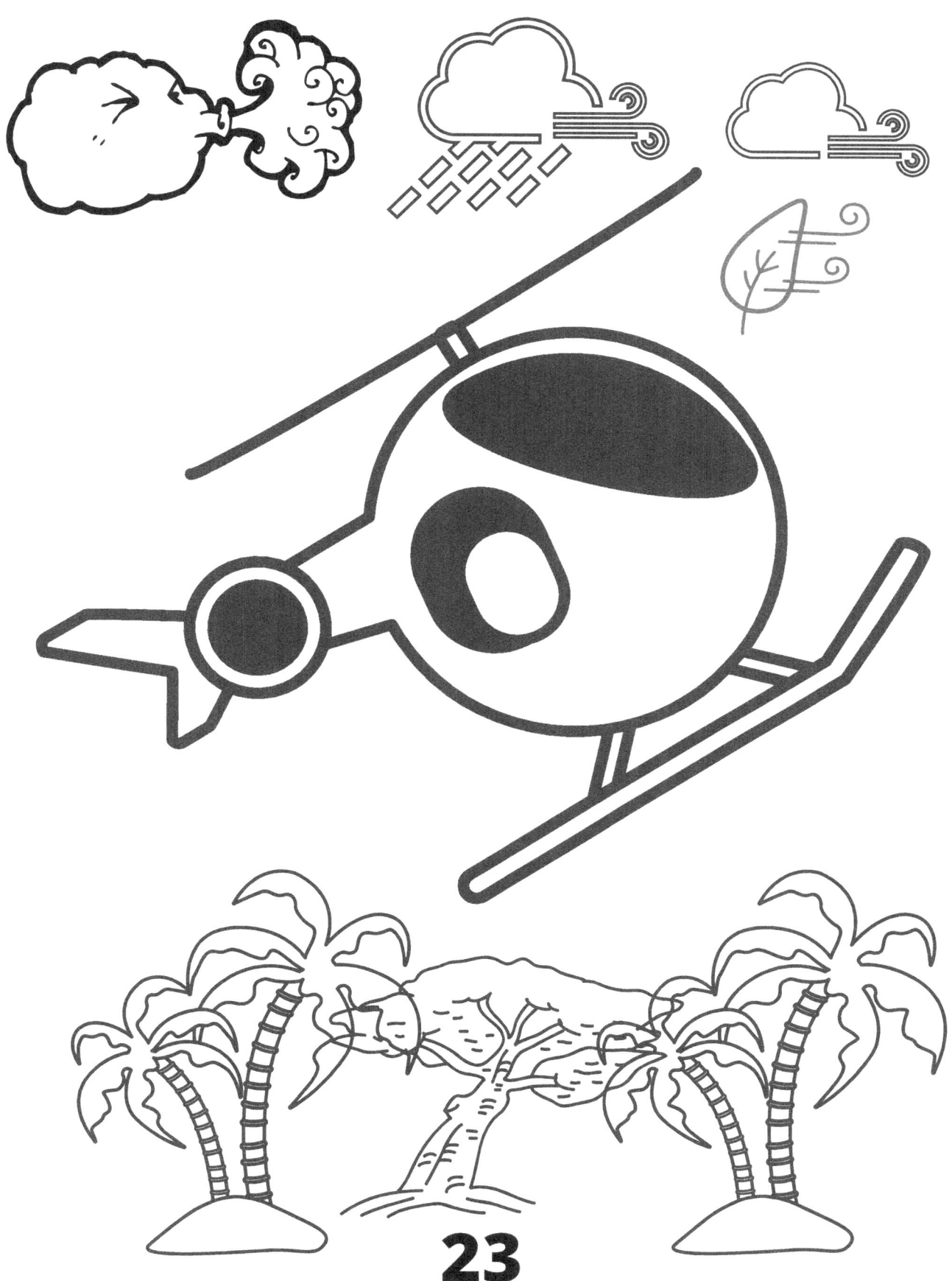

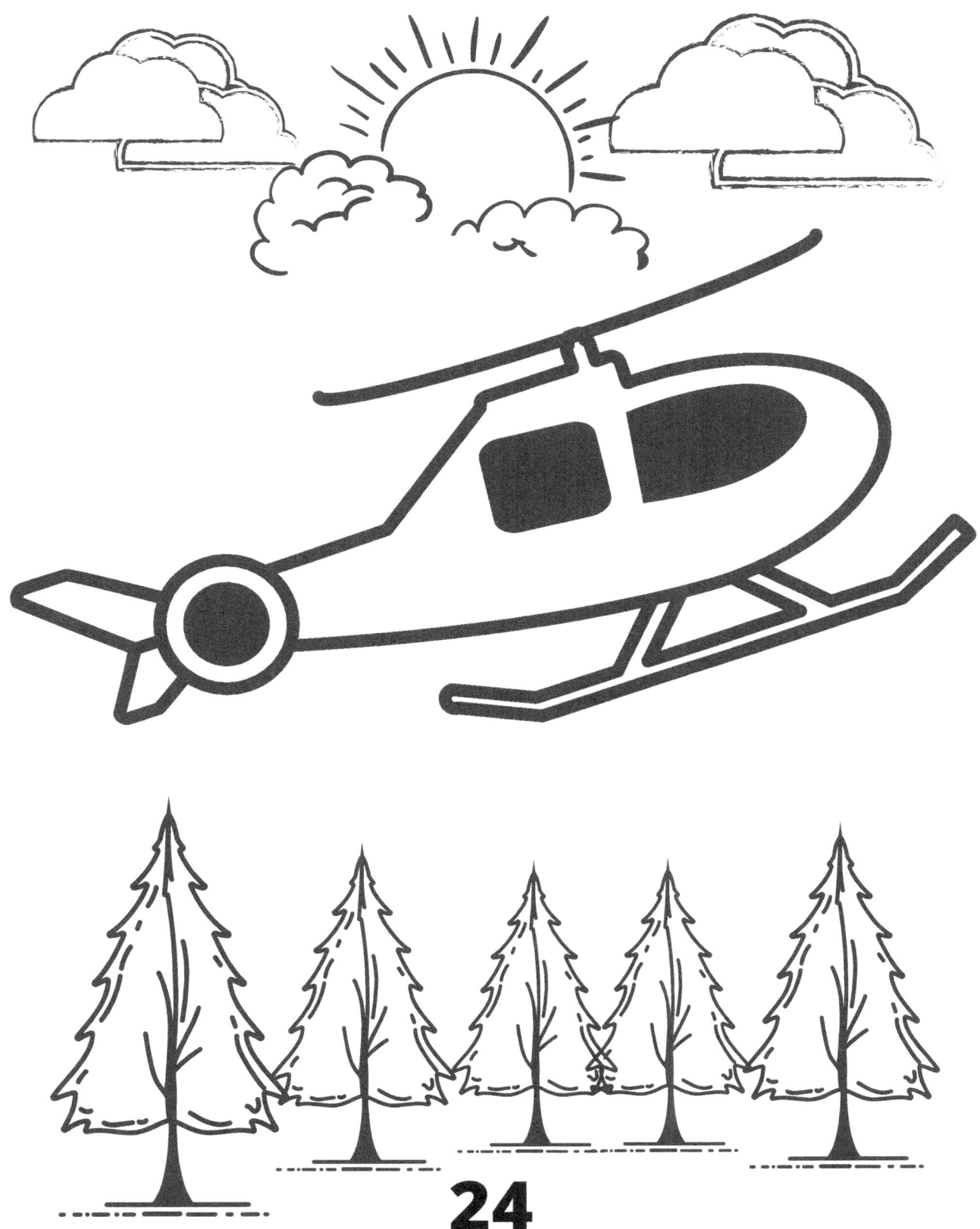

24

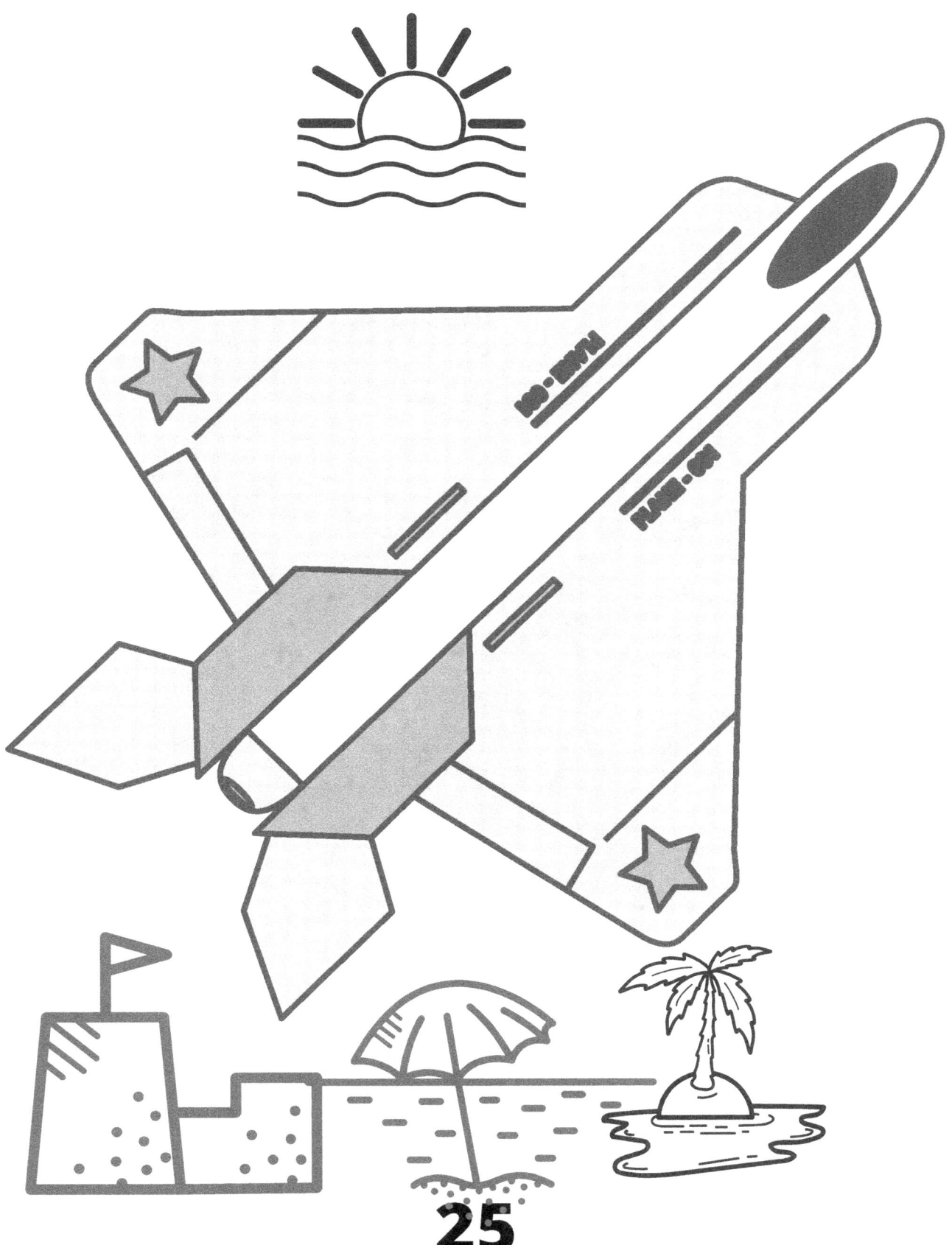

25

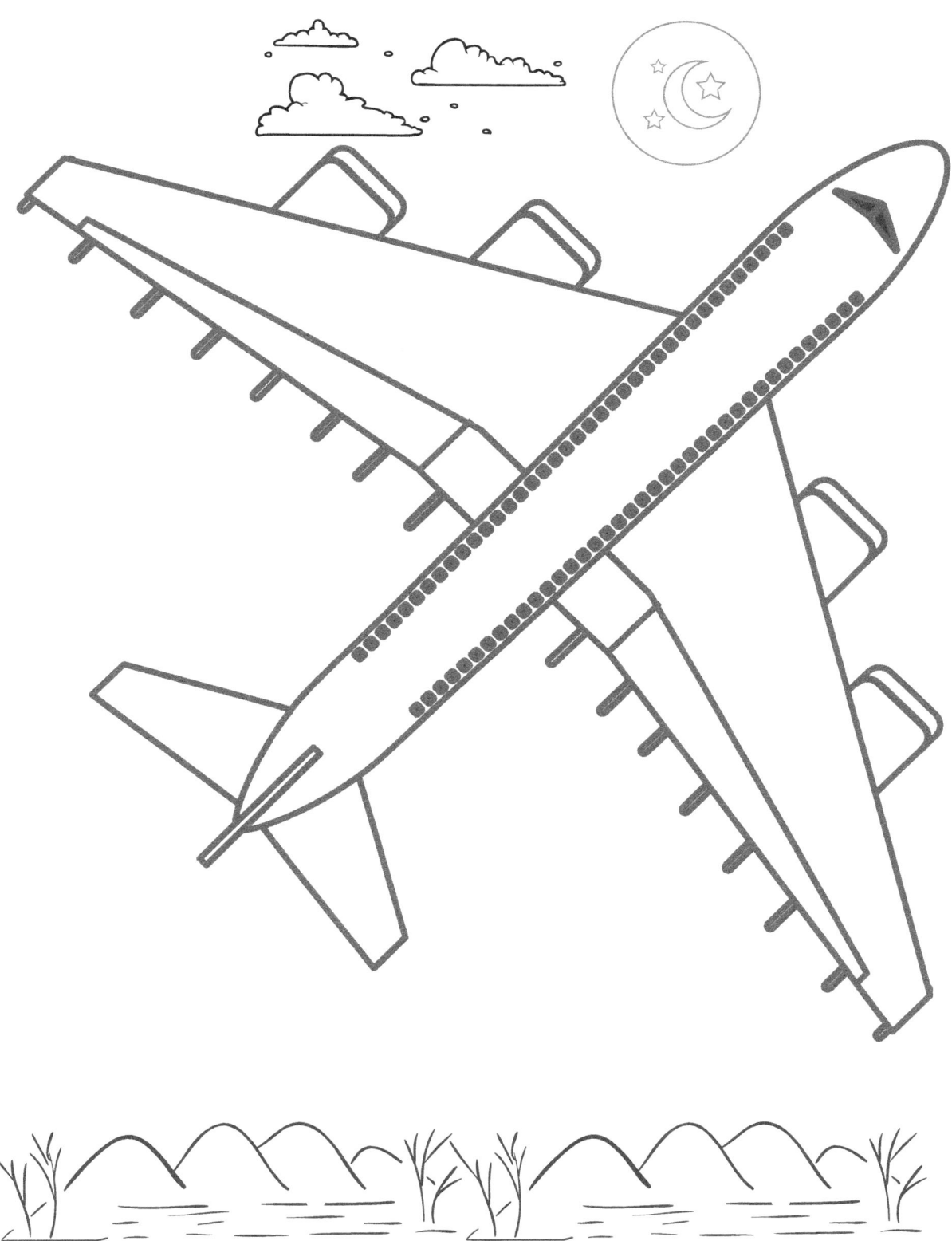

26

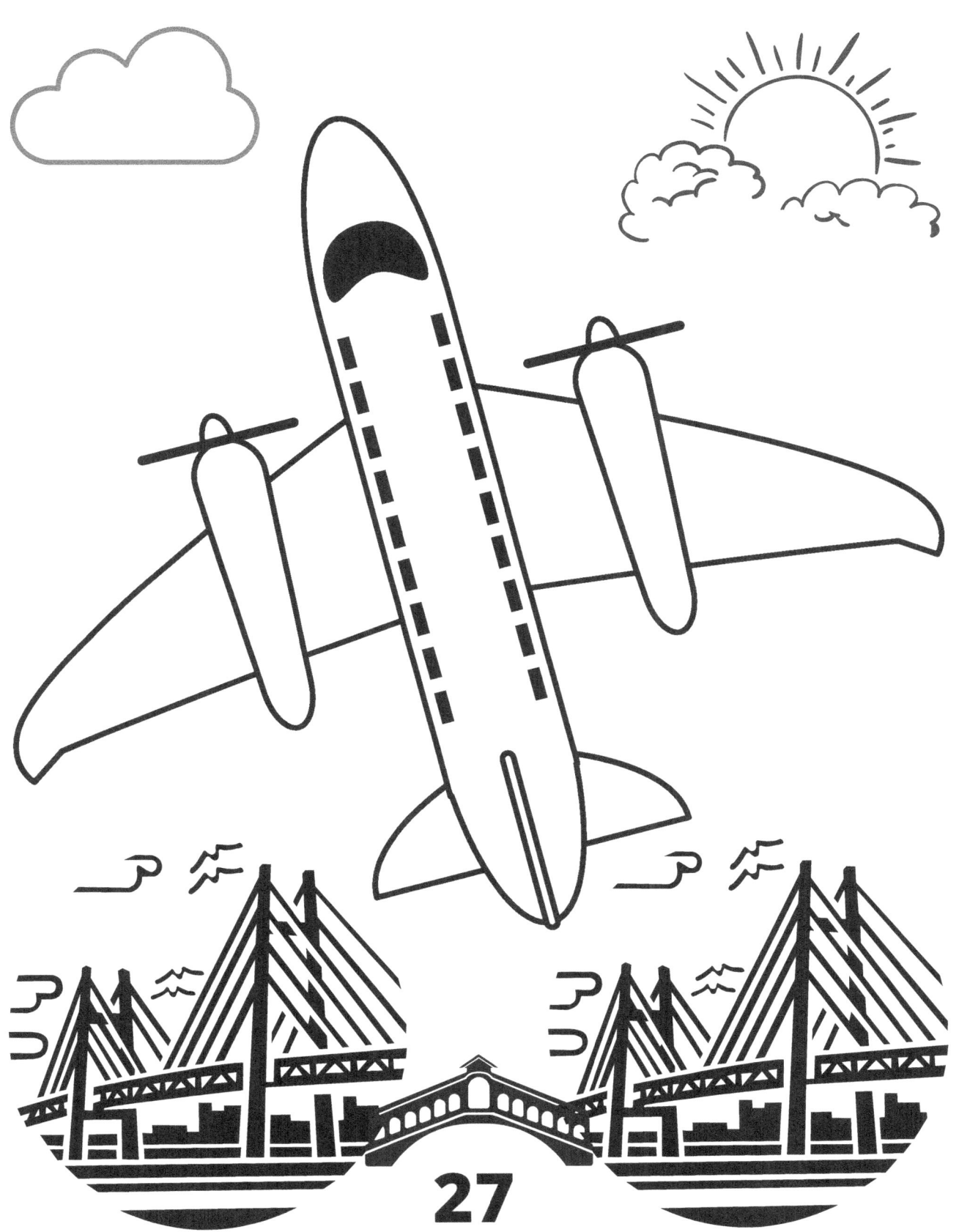

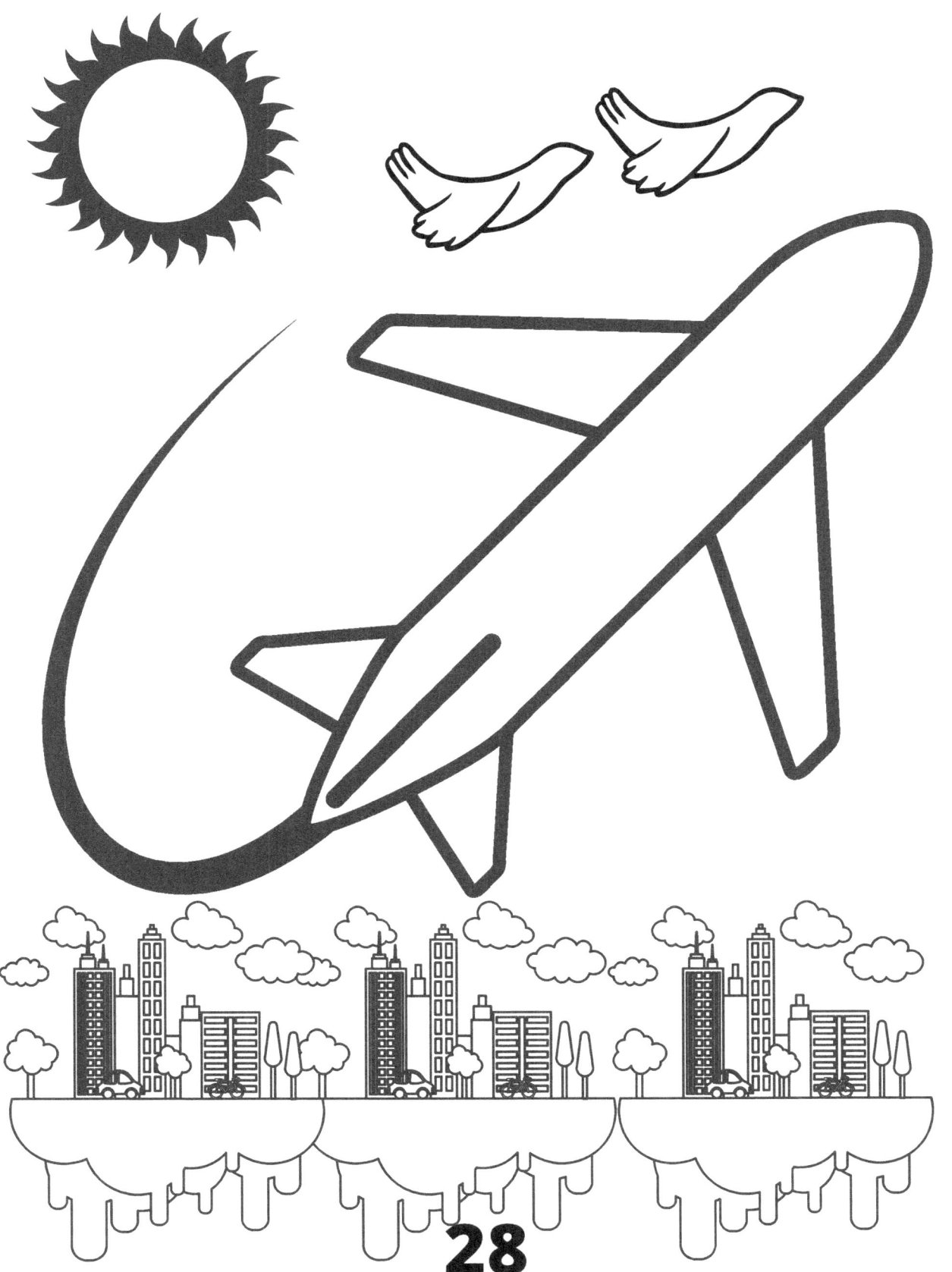

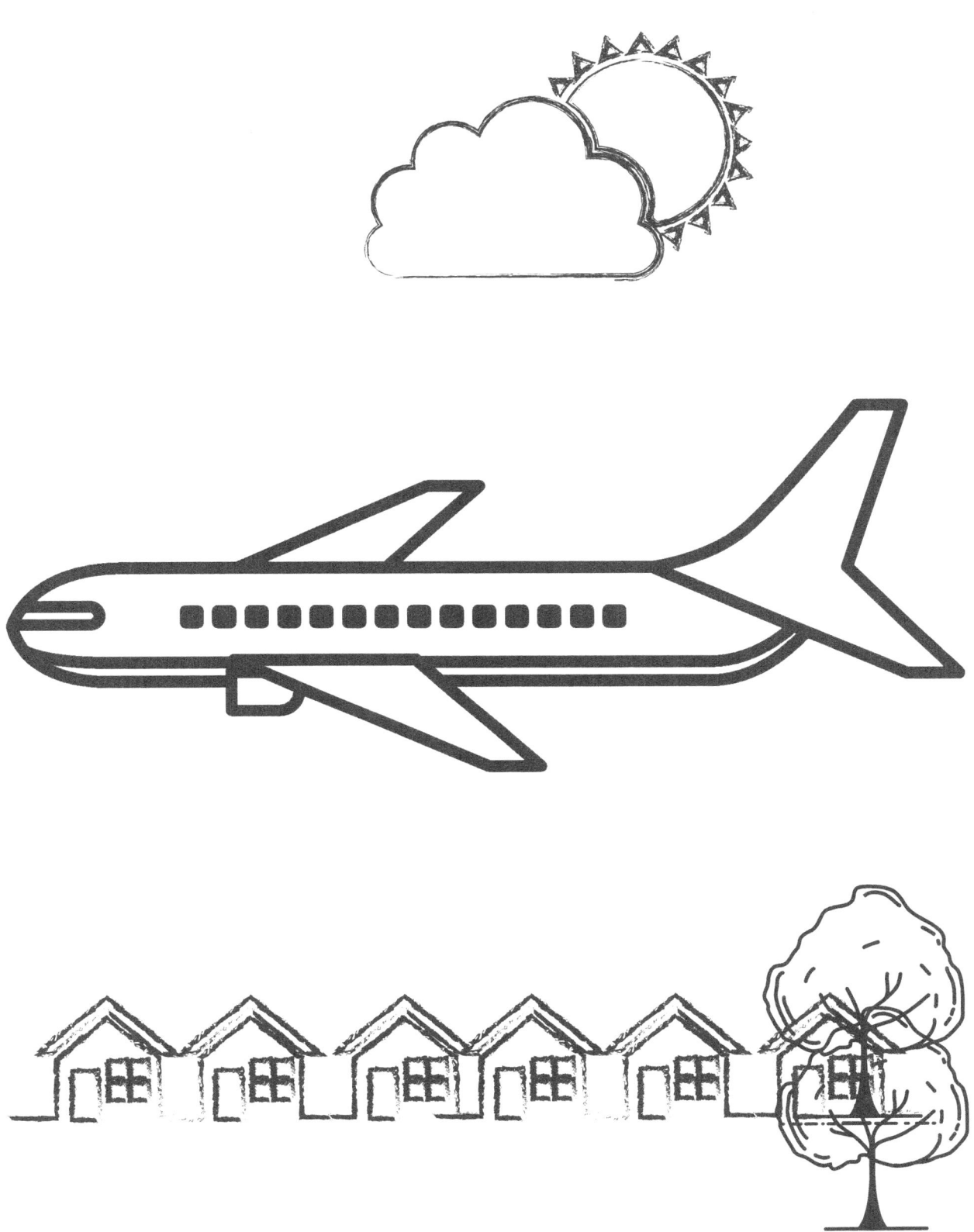

29

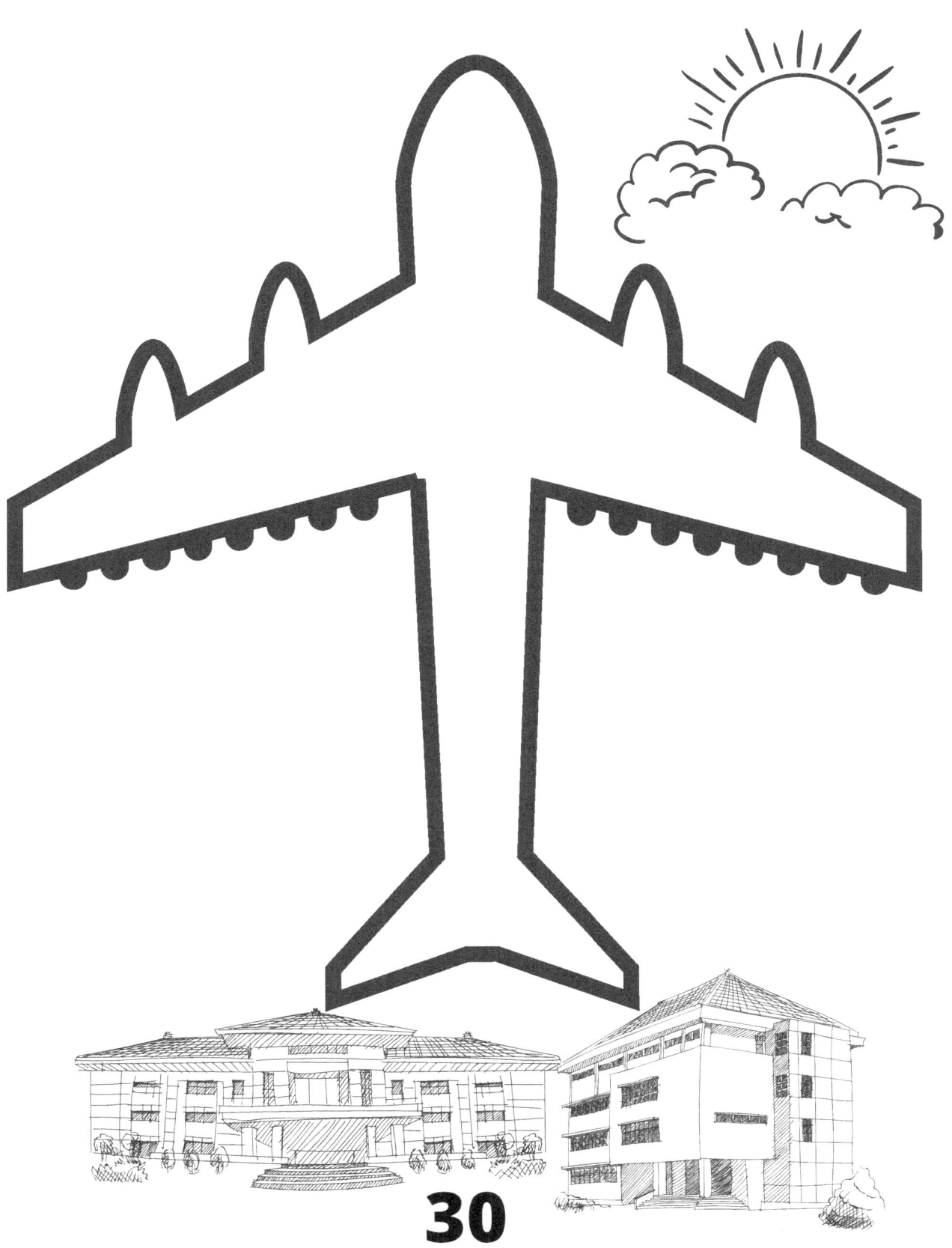

30

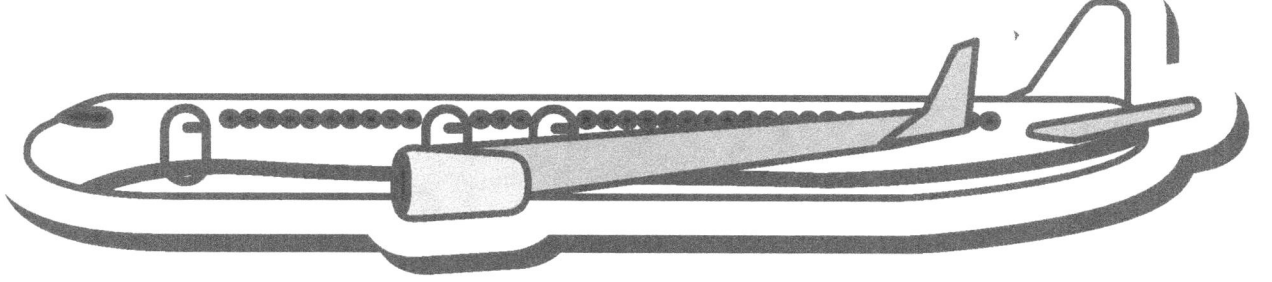

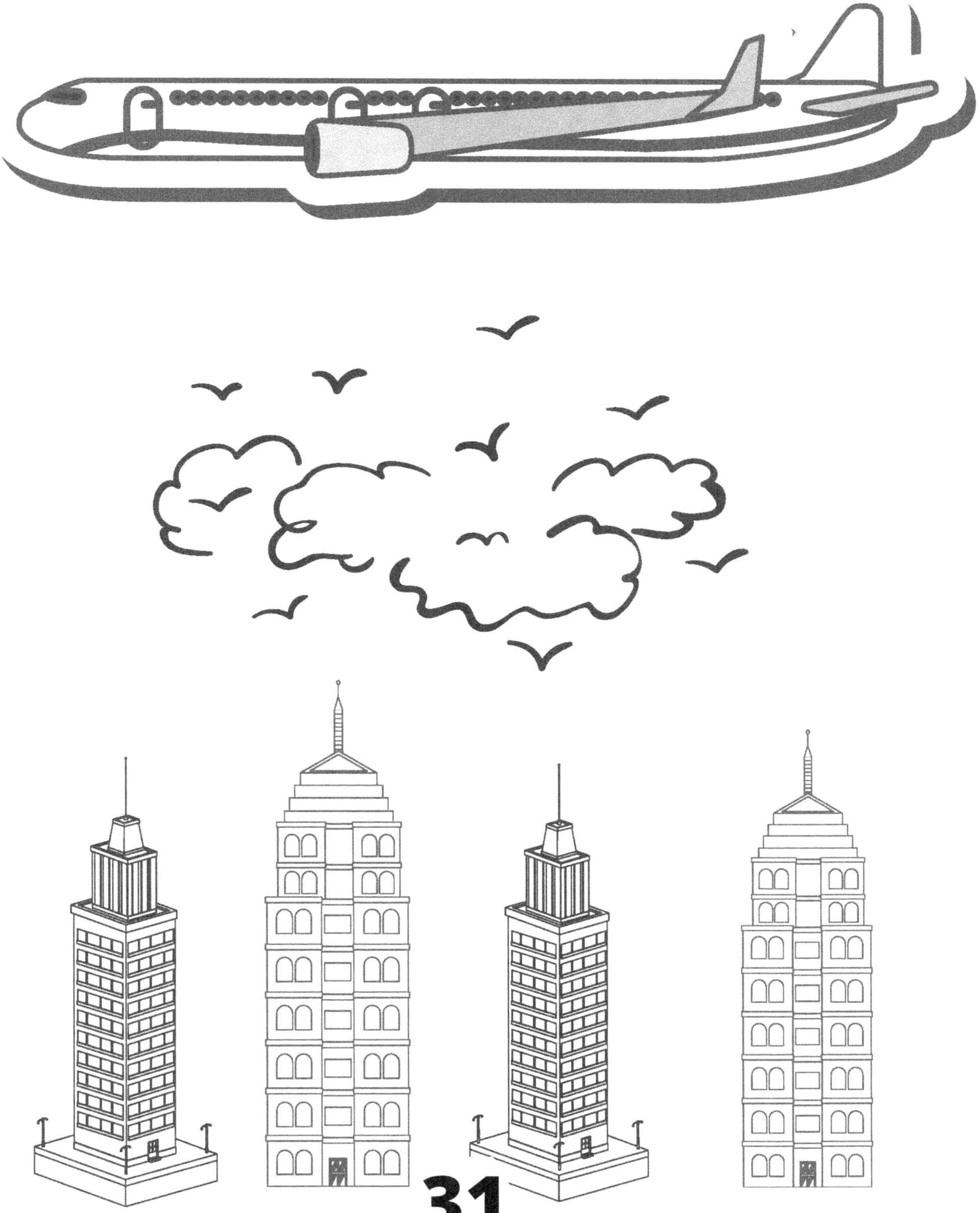

31

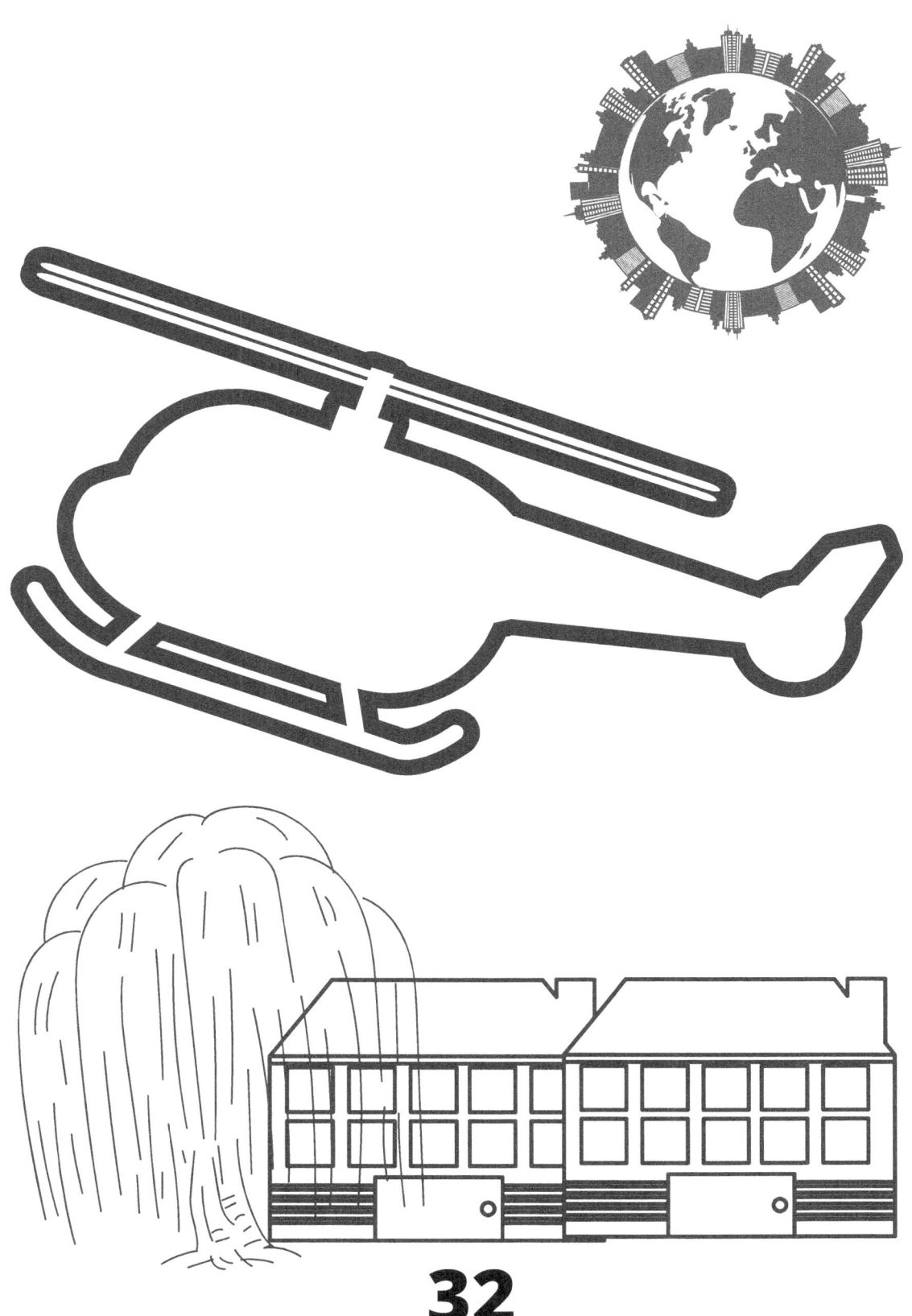

32

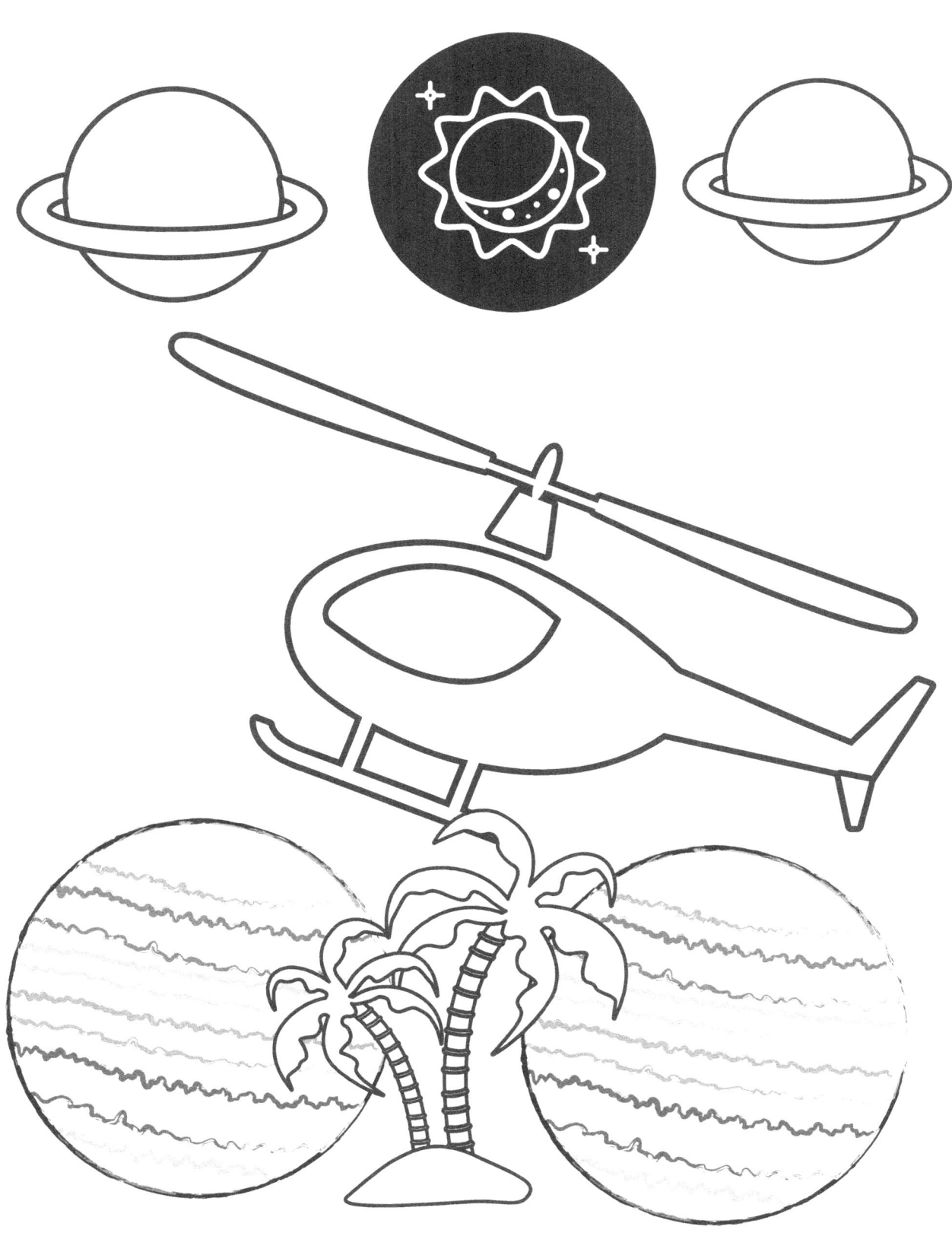

33

www.ingramcontent.com/pod-product-compliance
Lightning Source LLC
Chambersburg PA
CBHW080524220526
45465CB00006B/2594